BE THE GURU

A Step-By-Step Guide to Becoming Your Own Spiritual Teacher

GEORGE LIZOS

First published by George Lizos Limited, 2015
www.georgelizos.com

Copyright © George Lizos, 2015

The moral rights of the author have been asserted.

All rights reserved. No part of this publication may be reproduced, distributed, or transmitted in any form or by any means, including photocopying, recording, or other electronic or mechanical methods, without the prior written permission of the author, except in the case of brief quotations embodied in critical reviews and certain other non-commercial uses permitted by copyright law. For permission requests, write to the author at georgelizos@outlook.com.

None of the information in this book should substitute professional medical advice; the reader is advised to always consult a medical practitioner. The use of any information in this book is at the reader's risk and discretion, and the author cannot be held liable for its misuse.

ISBN: 978-1514180020

Cover Design: Fiaz Ahmed Irfan, Interior Design: Előd Csernik

Printed by CreateSpace

To me, for never giving up on my dreams.

TABLE OF CONTENTS

Introduction vii

PART I: AWAKEN THE GURU **1**

Chapter 1: A Tale Of Balls, Dreams And Daisies 3

Chapter 2: When Darkness Turns To Light 13

Chapter 3: The Most Powerful Law In The Universe . . 27

Chapter 4: Your Divine Self. 47

PART II: BECOME THE GURU **59**

Chapter 5: Self-Love Boot Camp. 61

Chapter 6: Radical Forgiveness. 79

Chapter 7: Your Body Knows Best 91

PART III: SECURE THE GURU **109**

Chapter 8: Dealing With Negative Experiences. 111

Chapter 9: Dealing With Negative People. 121

Chapter 10: Dealing With Negativity In The House . . 137

PART IV: EMPOWER THE GURU **153**

Chapter 11: Become A Master Manifestor........... 155

Chapter 12: Pay Your Intuition Fees 171

Chapter 13: Become A Messenger Of Heaven....... 189

Chapter 14: You Are The Guru 211

Keep Your Guru On 217

Acknowledgements 219

References..................................... 221

About the Author 222

INTRODUCTION
Read This First

Getting the Terms Right

The word *guru* means *teacher* in Sanskrit, and it is usually used to describe a spiritual teacher.

The word teacher comes from the Old English word *taecan*, which means "to show, point out, and to give instruction". It connotes someone who knows, and is the imparter of knowledge to other people. *Spiritual* means "of or concerning the spirit," and pertains to the quality of choosing to be in alignment with Spirit – God, Source, the Universe – by choosing to embody its primal quality of love, and to keep doing so. In this respect, spirituality is a never-ending process of becoming more and more in alignment with Spirit. When you combine the two terms, you get a spiritual teacher – a *guru*.

Although the guru's primary purpose is to teach, he understands that he is both a teacher and a student. He sees every single experience, and every person he interacts with, as an opportunity to learn, grow, and find alignment with the love that defines him (for simplicity purposes I will use the male pronoun through the book).

Why Be the Guru?

Being a spiritual teacher, or guru, is the ultimate form of self-empowerment. The guru is not dependent on anything or anyone for love, happiness, or wisdom. Any external source of these qualities is merely an addition to what he already knows, feels and practises.

The purpose of the guru is to find and thrive in his life purpose. The guru understands that every single person is born with a very specific mission that's crafted on his own unique blend of skills, talents and personality, which only he can accomplish. The guru knows that the key to succeeding in his life purpose is to maintain his alignment with love, and to have the courage to follow the guidance that comes as a result.

How to Be the Guru

You cannot become the guru, for you already *are* the guru. The purpose of this book is not to change you in any way, but to help you remember who you already are. You were born knowing your power and your purpose, but life's circumstances have caused you to stray away from your path.

My aim in writing this book is to guide you, step by step, to remember who you really are, to de-programme the limiting beliefs that prevent you from owning your Divine Self, and to ensure that you never stray away from it, so that you can follow and succeed in your purpose.

I believe that "experiences" are the ultimate form of teaching. For this reason, every chapter of this book will give you a palpable experience of the concepts discussed, so that you can draw your own conclusions and learn through your experience.

How to Use This Book

I've structured this book carefully, to guide you through the exact steps that you need to take to awaken, become, secure and empower your inner guru. As a result, for maximum benefits I suggest that you read the chapters in the order laid out.

More importantly, I suggest that you spend at least one week practising the processes in each chapter before moving on to the next one. This is an intensive course in spiritual awakening, and you may get overwhelmed if you overload your mind and schedule with too many concepts and processes at once.

Be the Guru is highly practical, and on many occasions I will ask you to take pen and paper and write things down. As a result, it will be beneficial to have a journal dedicated to this journey. Whether it is an electronic or a physical one, keeping all your processes in one place will help you keep track of your progress, and revisit practices when you need to.

Your Life Purpose

I've written this book as a response to people looking to find and succeed in their life purpose, and if you are reading this right now you are probably one of them. As a result, before we get started it is important that you have a clear awareness of what your life purpose is.

For this reason, I've created a step-by-step guide to help you discover it, which you can download here:

www.georgelizos.com/lifepurpose

PART I
AWAKEN THE GURU

In Part I you will awaken the guru that already lies dormant within you – Your Divine Self. Starting with my own personal story of awakening my own guru, I will introduce you to the most powerful law in the Universe – the Law of Attraction – and teach you how you can use it to manifest the perfect path for guiding you in this transformational journey. Most importantly, by the end of Part I you will have a personal, indisputable experience of your Divine Self, and will learn how to start transforming yourself into it.

Chapter 1

A TALE OF BALLS, DREAMS AND DAISIES

My mum always tells me how I grew up faster than most children. According to her I said my first "mama" at only two months old, and by the sixth month I could utter entire sentences. At my christening I had complete awareness of what was going on, so I peed on my godfather and screamed and cried for freedom all the way to the end. The childhood artefacts I found while digging up forgotten drawers and closets in our house in Cyprus – audio cassettes, toys, photo albums – and the few blurry memories I have all suggest that I was different from most children. I had a sense of maturity and seriousness that rendered me a loner amongst other children my age. I knew that I was here for a purpose, and I was just waiting for someone to hand me the instructions so that I could get to work.

My earliest childhood memory is of a three-year-old George standing all alone in what is plastered on my mind as hectares of yellow daisies, tending to my home-made garden and making little bouquets that I would use to decorate the entire house later that day. I never enjoyed socialising with other children in the neighbourhood, although I remember spying on them, bothered about being left out from all the fun. Despite my feelings, I never considered compromising who I was to gain access into their circle of what was, in my opinion, an immature and violent way of having fun. I was stubborn enough to stick to my guns until I found someone who shared the same interests as me.

However, not having a friend to share my passions with, and spending so much time alone at such a young age, inevitably gave birth to feelings of unworthiness. Even though I eventually found ways to enjoy myself, I longed for a time when I could do so with other like-minded people.

Kindergarten Surprises

This essence of loneliness also defined my kindergarten years, when my interest in flowers and gardening was expressed through the arts and crafts. Fortunately, my dad has saved a few of my kindergarten masterpieces of collages and sand paintings, some of which made it into children's art competitions. I had always been proud of my art projects, and they ended up being my main motivation for going to school every morning. Most boys in my year preferred playing football and other kinds of sports, but I personally considered all games involving a ball silly and pointless, and preferred hanging out with the girls, who were interested in more subtle activities, like drawing and singing.

The two girls I used to hang out with in kindergarten, Marina and Liza[1], kept me out of misery for the most part of my childhood. Our mums soon became friends, and I got to experience all the joy and fun I had longed for. They would arrange for us to go to parks and on other excursions, and at school we would always be together building sandcastles, constructing little houses for the ants in the school's garden, and being children in our own artsy way.

Fortunately, my mum sensed my sensitivities, and did everything in her power to provide a basis for my social integration, and to help me channel my natural interests. Even though I loved both of my parents, I had a special bond with my mum. Looking back to those days, my mum was the one I always depended on when I felt lost, and she was a constant loving presence at every stage of my life. She was there to share my happiness after I finished a drawing; she was my bodyguard when other boys bullied me; and she threw me absurd birthday parties that usually lasted a whole week and gained me hundreds of presents. In essence, my mum eased my transition into what seemed to be a harsh world of bullies and opportunists, and with her I always felt secure and content. I can say with confidence that had she not been in my life in those early years, I would probably still

---

[1] I gave them these pseudonyms to protect their privacy.

be that lonely child playing with the daisies in the back garden.

Primary School Traumas

Primary school[2] found me in a similar situation as kindergarten. I was naïve and bashful, living in my own airy-fairy bubble of unicorns and rainbows, and being the son and student parents and teachers longed for. In stark contrast, other kids my age were engaging in romantic relationships, smoking cigarettes, and doing the opposite of whatever their parents and teachers told them. I now realise that having no friends and being on my own for the most part of my childhood created an inner urge to please others, and be the person they wanted me to be, hoping that this would grant me acceptance into a society that constantly rejected me.

Rejection defined my early school years in most respects. As a result of my gentle and rather girly demeanour and interests, I didn't really enjoy hanging around with the other boys, who were interested in getting down and dirty, playing football and other macho games. I was more attracted to the girls' lifestyle and approach to having fun, which included taking walks around the school grounds and engaging in polite conversations. Unfortunately, the group of girls I liked to hang out with didn't seem to share the same opinion. Every single school break for at least four years I followed them

---

[2] This would be Elementary School in the US.

around the school hoping they would invite me to their group; and every single time they refused, sometimes even reporting me to a teacher for stalking them around.

Towards the end of primary school I gave up trying to be one of the girls and decided to give the boy thing a try. I was desperately trying to fit in somewhere – anywhere. As a result, I hesitantly made the decision to join the boys on the football pitch during the school breaks. Being the shy and reserved child I was, I didn't just dislike football; I was afraid of it. All the shouting, tripping over and running around, as well as the unpredictability of the game, were too much for me to handle, and so I took the least active position: defence.

Initially, playing in defence worked pretty well for me, since I had found the perfect balance between pretending to care about the game and not really doing much about it. I usually ran after the ball to show that I was trying to do something, but purposely never caught up to it. This formula worked, and I actually started getting some attention from the boys.

Unfortunately, everything went awry when my teammates decided one day that I was to be the goalkeeper. I remember my heart thumping faster and my breathing intensifying, solely at the idea of having a one-on-one contact with the ball. I did my best to hide my feelings from everybody else though – I had worked too hard for this, and there was no way I could ruin it.

Finally, the time came when an opposing team's player was rapidly approaching my way, completely undefended by my teammates. My heart was racing, and my desperation to prove myself completely took over me. I panicked, and before I realised it I was standing face to face with a shooting ball that ended up hitting me hard on the face. The pain was insurmountable, yet my team players were cheering at my "catching" of the ball, and nobody seemed to care about the fact that my face was red and swollen from the hit. It didn't seem to matter though, as I had finally managed to achieve the inconceivable: I had found the acceptance I longed for, and I was in hell.

Lost in Translation

Disappointed with myself and my decisions, I gave up on both boys and football, and went back to being the lonely, quiet geek I really was. While I pretended to be strong and proud in my loneliness, there was a war going on within me. Why was friendship so hard for me? Why couldn't I be like every other boy? Why was I different from everybody else? Why, why, why?! My mind was flooded with questions, and the pain was demolishing me.

In an attempt to understand what was wrong with me, I convinced myself that I was ugly and unattractive. Having slanted eyes and a darker complexion than everyone else was another aspect that made me stand out from my classmates, and I used this as an additional reason to justify my unpopularity. As a result of my self-inflicted misconceptions and unique demeanour, I became the perfect target for bullies. It was in these early teenage years of my life that I first became a victim to both psychological and physical bullying, marking the end of a strained childhood and the beginning of a sorrowful teenage-hood.

In time, I got used to both the derogatory comments and the occasional punches coming from older, brash guys; but what destroyed my self-esteem was the bullying coming from *me*. The dramas and traumas of my past had all worked together to lower my self-esteem, and convince me that there really was something wrong with me. Since I was just entering puberty and beginning to discover myself, my sexuality, and who I really was, I was vulnerable to other people's comments. Eventually, I came to share their opinion about me, pitying and bullying myself for being different and not fitting in.

What worsened the situation was the discovery of my sexuality, which was just beginning to shine through in my final year. Throughout the course of primary school I kept up with the relationship trend at the time, of picking a girl you felt some kind of attraction towards and pretending to "love" her (as is the expression used by most children of that age). My aim was to fit in, and since boys and girls generally decided to identify themselves with the labels of boyfriend and girlfriend, I participated. As with most of my attempts to blend in with the majority, this attempt also failed tragically following constant rejections from Lena, the girl I "loved" for the first four years of school. I didn't really care too much about the matter at the time, probably because I wasn't yet aware of my sexuality; and therefore I didn't *actually* have any romantic feelings towards her. As far as I was concerned, her rejection was similar to every other rejection I had gone through, and by that time I was used to them.

When I finally gave up on Lena, I moved on to another girl, Xenia, and pretended to love her in the same immature, childish way. At the same time, I started feeling drawn to my boy classmates. I remember enjoying hanging out in the boys' dormitories during breaks, eyeing up younger boys, and staring at my classmates while playing football or changing clothes after PE. The thought of being gay hadn't crossed my mind then, because I didn't even know what being gay meant. Nobody had told me that there was even a possibility of two boys falling in love; and being the timid child I was, I never asked anyone about it. As a result, I had no possible explanation for this seemingly unique interest of mine. I didn't know what it was, or why it was happening, so I kept it hidden from everyone else and carried on with loving, and getting rejected by, Xenia.

My primary school years ended in the same way they had started. I was still the same lonesome child with no real friends, feeling belittled and unworthy. On top of that, I had gained a lot of weight and had no sense about who I was or what my sexuality was. Instead of finding myself,

I completely lost it; and the only things I was proud of were my achievements in school, my involvement in the arts, and an acceptance into one of the best private high schools in Cyprus, which I hoped would give me everything that primary school hadn't.

Chapter 2

WHEN DARKNESS TURNS TO LIGHT

I went into high school with an unfazed diligence, aiming to transform my life. Fortunately, there would be no one there from my previous school to inform my new classmates of my introverted weirdness, and the shameful experiences that defined my primary-school era. It was the perfect opportunity for me to start over with a clean slate, and I couldn't have been happier about it.

I was determined to overcome my insecurities and be more sociable, to try different things, and to mingle with different groups of people until I found the one I fitted in the best. The expectation of change, and excitement for a new beginning, led to a perfect unfolding of the first few months. I quickly made new friends, and I no longer wandered around the schoolyard like a lost puppy during breaks. I was surrounded by high-achievers, so nobody made fun of me for doing well at school, and I successfully managed to join the school's music society as a member of the choir. My confidence level was rising fast.

Unfortunately, a few more months into the year and my school life took a completely different turn. I remember lunching and socialising with a friend at the school's backyard during a break when a boy in my class came up to me. "Hey George, are you straight?" he asked in a snickering way. Alex, the boy I was hanging out with, urged me to say no; but since I had no idea what the question really meant, I ignored him. "What does straight mean?" I asked vacantly; and I watched as he and his friends burst into laughter and walked away. Befuddled, I turned to Alex, wondering what that was all about. "Straight means not gay," he explained to me politely on our way back to class.

Such was my innocence and sexual ignorance at the age of 12 that I simply had no idea of what gay meant. Sex was not really a subject I talked about with my parents, and I'd had no close friends in my past to inform me about the different sexual terms. As far as I was concerned, sex was a forbidden word only spoken by adults, and gays were criminals of the worst kind – even the word was strictly avoided. That being so, why would someone ask me if I was not-gay? Of course I was straight. I had always been polite to people, had abided by the rules my parents set for me, and was one of the best students at school. Crime was not even a word in my vocabulary. How could I be gay, then?

That day I returned home eager to learn everything I could about sex and gays. I searched my parents' bookcase and found a book called *The Encyclopedia of Marriage*. Surprised I hadn't noticed the book before, I spent the entire day devouring its contents and absorbing all the information about sex that I could find. I couldn't believe how unaware I was about everything. A sense of shame took over me as I realised that I was living in a bubble of ignorance, while everyone around me was having secret sex – or so I thought. Unfortunately, the word "gay" didn't seem to pop up anywhere in the book, so I had to bring in the big guns.

We didn't have Internet at home at the time, so on my next visit to my dad's office on a Saturday afternoon, I secretly logged into a PC, typed the keyword in the search bar, and pressed Search.

And then everything went silent.

I was faced with hundreds upon hundreds of pictures of men engaging erotically in activities I had never seen before, and didn't even know were possible. At that moment a surge of realisation came over me, and my body was paralysed. I felt my skin numbing and my blood freezing as I stared at the computer screen, puzzled and terrified. It felt as if time had frozen and I was trapped lingering between two different worlds: the pure and innocent world of my childhood, and the treacherous and cruel world of everyone else.

As the shock subsided and I became accustomed to the pictures, my mind was flooded with all kinds of questions. Why were those men having sex? Wasn't sex supposed to be between a man and a woman? Was sex between men legal? Were there many gay people around the world? Why hadn't I met any gay people or couples in Cyprus? Why was that boy asking me whether I was straight? What made him ask that question? Was I acting in a way that made me look gay? Most importantly – was I gay? The questions were too many to handle in one session, so I logged myself off and went on with my day, only to return the next week and repeat the process all over again.

I might not have had an answer to all the questions befuddling my mind at the time, but one thing was certain – I had enjoyed looking at the pictures.

...

The first year of high school went by pretty uneventfully. By the end of it I informed myself thoroughly on the subject of sex, including homosexuality; and even though I delved into a bit of a Googling once in a while, I refused to associate myself with any gay activity. After all, my parents and society had made sure to shape my beliefs in a way that associated homosexuality with a negative and hostile connotation; and being the perfect figure of a son that I was, I had to stay away from it.

Concurrently, my natural gay urges were gradually overpowering every single rule and belief I had, and I couldn't resist fantasising about other boys at school. *As long as nobody knows about it, it's OK*, I thought.

The Boot Camp

Things took a radical turn the next summer when my classmates' derogatory comments intensified, making me conscious of my effeminate characteristics. At the time, I was obsessed with a daily TV music show that held a competition every weekend. I spent every week watching the show and taking notes on the topics discussed, hoping that they would choose me as a participant. When I finally got accepted, I prepared my notes and waited eagerly by the telephone, waiting for the anticipated call. To my surprise, the competition went great, and I even managed to win the prize I had hoped for. What I didn't expect was to listen back to the recording and hear myself talking in what seemed to me like an incredibly feminine way. Was that how I always talked? How had I not realised it?

Ashamed of myself, I ran to my room and burst into tears. I was just beginning to realise that I *was* gay, but there was no way I would admit that to anyone else or myself. I couldn't be gay! What would my parents think when they found out? What would society think? People would make fun of me. My childhood and primary-school experiences had led me to believe that I had to earn my worthiness from the people around me. Therefore, I always did everything in my power to satisfy the people in my life. How could I believe differently? I had always been the outcast, the loner, the bashful boy who played with flowers, loved singing and hated football. I was also fat, had strange facial characteristics, and wore braces. Adding the word "gay" to my attributes would destroy any chances I had to thrive at school and in life.

As a result, in the following two years I put myself into a mental boot camp designed to modify all aspects of myself that could assign me the gay label. I began practising my walking in front of the mirror, and making sure there was no wiggling that could signify that I was queer. I watched my hand movements and facial expressions, trying to keep them blunt and rigid, and avoided over-enthusiastic expressions. As a result, I began walking in a really weird and robot-like way that made me look handicapped; but as long as it didn't make me look gay, that was fine with me. When it came to talking, I found it pretty hard to modify the way I expressed myself, since hearing myself on TV made me realise that we sound to other people differently to what we do to ourselves.

Despite all my effort, the derogatory comments and bullying towards me got even more intense, leading me to the conscious decision to not talk to people at all. I figured that if I abstained from talking, they wouldn't have any excuse to pick on me. As a result, I distanced myself from the few friends I had, and returned back to my loner primary-school routine of wandering alone around the school and going to the library during breaks, because I had nothing else to do and nobody to talk to.

With all the self-policing, I became more conscious about the way I looked, too. I never really liked my appearance; probably because ever since I remember people always commented on how different I was from everyone else, whereas all I wanted was to blend in and be normal. I remember crying myself to sleep almost every night, dreading another day in my overweight body and miserable life.

As a result, on the summer before my first year of high school I decided to lose that weight once and for all. This was my last attempt to change myself, hoping it would grant me the key to normality and help me gain the acceptance I so desperately longed for. That summer I starved myself to the point that I was on the verge of anorexia. My compulsive perfectionism, hunger for love, and a multitude of complexes had all combined to turn my diet into an obsession, until my mum had to force me to go to a nutritionist, who immediately got me on a weight-gain diet.

Equipped with my new, socially acceptable body, I went through the fourth year of high school with high expectations. Even though I was still unsociable and talked and acted in a bizarre way, I managed to lose my pounds of pain and obscure all signs that would render me a homosexual; or so I thought. Unfortunately, despite all my hard work, the bullying got even more intense and hostile; and apart from the usual demeaning comments I would get during breaks, my boy classmates also bullied me in class too, in front of my teachers and all my classmates.

As if bullying at school wasn't enough, I was fighting an even harsher battle at home – with myself. Despite all the external changes I had forced onto me, there was little I could do about the way I felt towards other boys. It was becoming clear to me that my gayness was there to stay, but I refused to accept that. Consequently, I kept affirming that I was going through puberty and the "gay thing" was just a phase I was going through. I even forced myself to fantasise about women, and avoided looking at men altogether, hoping to "cure" myself from the "disease" that society said homosexuality was.

On top of my fighting on two fronts at the same time, my family life got more intense. My parents got divorced, which made the relationship between them even more hostile than it was before, and they were fighting over how many hours my brother and I were to spend with each one of them. Of course, our opinion didn't really matter, and they juggled us around, completely ignoring our personal preferences. As if the topsy-turvydom of my life wasn't enough, I now had to deal with my parents' insecurities, and try to please them even more.

My life got harder and harder, and I was running out of options. All I had ever wished for was to be able to live a normal life like everyone else, and fit in without always standing out. I didn't want to be different. I was tired of being every bully's victim, I was fed up with being alone, and I wanted to enjoy my life just like any other teenager of my age.

In what will always stay in my mind as a dark and cold night, I found myself crying in my room, tortured over my life's failures. I was at a point where everything I had tried failed, and despite all my efforts my life had only got worse. I had done everything I could to change everything about my body, the way I walked and talked, my interests, my feelings, my desires, and my sexuality. I tried to be the best student I could be, and to give my parents the perfect son they wished for – and yet nothing was enough. I came to the conclusion that I was a human abomination – a sick person who would never be the stereotype that society expected me to be.

My eyes stung with tears as I picked up a piece of paper and a pen and started scribbling down: "I'm sorry for what I did. I just can't live with myself anymore... this way. I've tried to change but I couldn't. I can't. I want you to know that I love you and I'm sorry." I gently let the pen down and picked up the small plastic box I had stolen from the first-aid kit moments before. I pulled out the pill case and came face to face with my future. I popped a few pills out and hesitantly threw them into my mouth. I felt empty and liberated at the same time, as I took the glass of water from my desk and took a large sip.

Coming to Light

Tears swelled up my eyes and I burst into an irrepressible weeping, trying to muffle my voice in the pillow. I went for the rest of the pills, but before I could pop them into my mouth I was hit by a realisation that forced me to pause.

"What are you doing!?" I asked myself intently, and immediately regretted taking the first two pills. I didn't know who or what was behind my radical change of outlook, but at that instant the solution to all my problems became clear. As I look back on this moment now, I realise that only when I had released all resistance could I receive a clear and vivid solution to what I'd been going through. Paradoxically, my decision to end my life got me to that state.

In seconds, what could have been a tragic night transformed into one of the most empowering nights of my life, as I finally made the conscious decision to accept who I was and embrace my homosexuality. All the need to be perfect, to abide by society's stereotypes, to be accepted by my parents and classmates, and to change who I was, had miraculously subsided; and I told myself that from that point on, I would focus all my energy on healing and empowering myself.

I was fifteen years old at the time, and in the following years I delved into a transformative path of love and self-empowerment, as I searched for tools and concepts that could reunite me with my Divine Self, and heal my life from all the drama I had put myself through. I knew that it would be a long ride that would require me to confront some of my most painful childhood traumas, but I was ready for it. I had been to the bottom so many times that there was no other path for me to take, than to rise from the ashes like a true phoenix and become the person who I knew lay hidden inside me.

Being interested in metaphysics from a young age, I found the path of spirituality to be the most logical path to take for my healing. What triggered my interest in metaphysics and nurtured my motivation for self-discovery were the Harry Potter books and movies. I had already been well into the books, and I loved how JK Rowling melded the powers of magic and love in such a beautiful way. These two concepts filled the inner child within me with hope and possibility, and gave me the formula I needed to embark on a transformational journey.

The books inspired me to search for real-life teachings of this formula, and in the following years I read every book on the topics of spirituality and metaphysics that I could get my hands on. With every book I read I felt stronger; and every new modality I learned about helped me deal with my past traumas and create my new self.

My self-acceptance and inner transformation brought miraculous changes in every aspect of my life. I smiled more, talked and walked with confidence, and wore my gayness with pride. My self-confidence soared to the sky, and I no longer cared about what other people thought about me. Moreover, my self-love became magnetic, and I started attracting friends and people who loved me and accepted me for the person I was. As a result, I graduated from high school as an entirely different person, with all the hopes and dreams of my years of struggle being fulfilled in ways I could never have imagined.

Becoming the Guru

After high school, I was guided to keep pushing the envelope of my spiritual awakening, and I went on to study a variety of spiritual modalities. In 2010 I did a Bachelor's degree in Metaphysical Sciences, which gave me an all-round education in metaphysics. In the same year I also became a Reiki Master, and delved into *The Teachings of Abraham*, Louise Hay, and the Law of Attraction. Afterwards, I took courses in astral projection, mediumship, and angel healing, and became a student of *A Course In Miracles*.

If I had to describe my spiritual journey in one word this would be self-empowerment. What my life experience helped me understand – which is the primary teaching of this book – is that there is nothing more liberating than being your own source of love and happiness. In my life I never had the comfort of being loved, empowered, appreciated, or depending on anyone for emotional support. As a result, I had to work harder and learn how to be my own source of love and acceptance. In hindsight, I know that my soul chose to go through these experiences to afford me with this lesson, so that I could teach it to others.

As a result, the purpose of my spiritual journey was to learn tools, processes and modalities that freed me from co-dependency, and allowed me to be my own guru. *Be the Guru* is the culmination of my journey up until this present moment. It is my manifesto and formula for finding the ultimate form of self-empowerment. Modelled on my personal journey, and practised by my one-on-one coaching clients, it will provide you with a step-by-step guide to becoming the guru that lies within you.

Chapter 3

THE MOST POWERFUL LAW IN THE UNIVERSE

Over the past decade, the Law of Attraction has enjoyed tremendous popularity in the media, especially after the release of the book and movie *The Secret*. As a result, more and more people have been awakened to their creative potential, to manifest their desires and turn their lives around.

Like many people, I also discovered the Law of Attraction through *The Secret*. At the time, I was already taking conscious steps to improve my life through a variety of metaphysical modalities, particularly Western Feng Shui. Even though Feng Shui worked pretty well for me and I experienced tremendous improvements in my life, I always wondered what drove its workings. It wasn't until I discovered the Law of Attraction that everything made sense. With every page of *The Secret* that I read, I was imbued with a new revelation, and all my life's pitfalls started making sense. Awakened to its liberating truth, I felt as if I had returned home after years of fighting a brutal war, and I was finally free to start living the life I deserved.

I realised that the Law of Attraction was the most powerful law in this universe, and the foundation for transforming my life. As a result, I made it my utmost goal to study and master it, until I was living and breathing its teachings. Years of trial and error later, and having practised hundreds of different processes, I managed to get the hang of it. Not only did I manage to completely renovate my life and manifest my everyday desires, but I also attracted the perfect blend of teachings, concepts, and processes that I needed to become my own guru – hence the birth of this book.

Today, I consider the Law of Attraction to be the most basic and fundamental concept for becoming your own guru, because it provides you with the formula upon which everything in life is created, as well as the wherewithal to attract the necessary information, skills, and experiences, to awaken your Divine Self.

What is the Law of Attraction?

"Like attracts like." These three words capture the essence of the Law of Attraction. They suggest that whatever you believe in becomes true for you, and whatever you give out comes back to you. It is a simple concept to understand, yet you may have a hard time accepting it, and living by it. That's because you grew up in an action-oriented world, where your parents, teachers, and the whole of society taught you that the only way you could be successful was if you struggled and worked hard. How can you all of a sudden disregard a belief system you've nurtured and lived by for so many years, and place your faith in a wishy-washy metaphysical law?

That was exactly my initial response when I first found out about the Law of Attraction, and I knew that unless I found convincing evidence of its workings, I couldn't trust it completely.

Even though the movie and book of *The Secret* did a great job in providing practical processes to apply the Law of Attraction in different aspects of life, I personally found that they lacked a deeper explanation of the underlying mechanism that made the attraction possible. What is it about our thoughts and beliefs that attract *like* experiences? What triggers the attraction process? I knew that there was something more meaningful and existential behind the simplistic definitions, and I was determined to find it.

How Does the Law of Attraction Work?

It wasn't until I dug into the (well-disguised) scientific studies about the Law of Attraction that I discovered the evidence I was looking for. It seems that, since most of the Law of Attraction books in publication today are oriented towards the masses, they purposely exclude the ontological information that forms the basis of the Law's workings. While it was hard to extract the essence behind complicated mathematical formulae and quantum physics theories, my determination to get to the bottom of it, along with some precious help from my physicist friends, led me to the degree of detail and understanding that I sought.

Thankfully for you, you won't have to go through this time-consuming process, because I've summarised my main findings in a few simple and understandable points:

- **Everything is vibration:** Everything in your life, our world and the Universe, physical or non-physical, living or inanimate – even your thoughts – is energy, and energy is vibration.

- **Vibration attracts:** Everything in the universe vibrates at different frequencies; and forms with similar vibrational frequency are attracted to each other.

- **We are interconnected:** Think of the Universe as a huge vibrational spider's web where each connecting point represents a form of consciousness – humans, animals, trees, mountains, inanimate objects, and every single part of our universe. They are all individual points, but they are all connected to each other as part of one single system. Even though every form of consciousness vibrates at a different frequency, they all have the same basic vibrational core, which is why they are interconnected. Visualise this web as a symphony orchestra with each instrument playing a different tune. Even though the tunes are different, they all harmonise together into a single polyphonic, and symphonic, piece of music.

- **Law of Attraction:** Our interconnectivity grants you access to everything that's part of this web, provided that you manage to vibrate at the particular frequency of whatever it is you want.

Emotional GPS

The above model provides you with a conceptual understanding of the mechanism that drives the Law of Attraction. However, you may still wonder: How does this understanding translate into human terms? How can you change your vibration? More importantly, how can you match your vibrational frequency to the vibrational frequency of your desires?

Let me clarify it for you:

- Your indication for vibration is emotion, because your moment-to-moment emotions are directly proportional to the vibrational frequency you emit.

- Your emotions range from negative to positive. At the negative side lie fear and depression; and at the positive side, love and happiness. In between the two ends are all the other emotions, each one vibrating at a different frequency.

- Positive emotions have a high vibrational frequency, and negative emotions have a low vibrational frequency.

- In order to attract something into your life you need to find the vibrational frequency that matches the vibrational frequency of *having* what you desire.

- Since your vibrational frequency is directly related to your emotions, then the vibrational frequency of *having* something is synonymous to positive emotions like joy, appreciation and empowerment – the emotions you would have, had you already owned your manifested desires.

- Therefore, in order to find and embody the vibrational frequency of that which you want, you have to trick yourself into *feeling* that what you desire is already part of your life. That is, to find and embody the emotional signature of your desire.

- Your emotions act like a GPS, giving you constant evidence of where you stand in relation to the emotion linked to having your manifested desire.

Thoughts vs. emotions

The reason most books on the Law of Attraction state that it is your thoughts, rather than your emotions, that create your life, is simply because emotions are created by thoughts. Whatever you feel at any particular time is backed by a specific thought – or a combination of thoughts or beliefs – which trigger that particular emotion.

In this respect, your thoughts involve the asking for a desire, and your emotions the attracting of it. The basis behind thoughts as the main attracting mechanism is that we are verbal beings who have invented hundreds of words, and therefore thoughts, to express our emotions. As a result, your thoughts provide you with an accurate, indirect link to your emotions, and therefore to your vibrational frequency.

Practising the Law of Attraction

Employing your emotional GPS to align yourself with your desires is simple in theory, but it can get a bit tricky when you try to put it into practice. Finding the emotional signature of your desires calls for unequivocal certainty that what you desire is already part of your life. "Fake it till you make it" is an accurate and powerful teaching slogan, but how simple is it to convince yourself that you already live, or have, something that has nothing to do with your current circumstances?

Manifestation processes falling into the fake-it-till-you-make-it category include visualisation, scripting, and doing positive affirmations, as well as the simple act of living the lie until it becomes your reality. However, whereas living life in denial is attainable for a trained mind, it just isn't a sustainable way of going about any kind of manifestation; and even if the initial exhilaration from these processes gives you a kick start, after a few days you will get tired of the pretence and give up.

As a result, I've designed a manifestation process that excludes such processes, and offers a more effortless way to manifest your desires. Before I share it with you, though, let's first get some basic definitions down.

Types of desires

There are two types of human desires: Instinctive and Intentional ones.

- **Instinctive:** Instinctive desires arise whenever you find yourself in an unwanted situation. In the face of negativity you habitually ask for an improved version of what you have experienced. For example, if you come down with the flu, your body will instantly ask for health; when you struggle financially you immediately ask for financial remuneration; and when you get into a fight with a friend you instinctively ask for ease and understanding. In other words, negativity causes you to ask; and even if you don't verbalise, or think about, your desires, they are instinctively set into motion.

- **Intentional:** These are the kinds of desires that you deliberately set forth when you dream and think about your life and future. They are intentional because they represent your need for something that isn't directly related to an unwanted situation. You set forth intentional desires when you dream about your ideal mate, the perfect car, your dream job, or a promotion at work.

Your vibrational safe

Whenever you intentionally or instinctively desire something, God, Spirit, Source, the Universe – whatever you want to call it (I will use these terms interchangeably through the book) – instantly grants you its manifestation. Your desires first manifest in a vibrational form, and they only become physical when you embody their emotional signature. In other words, the reason you aren't living your desires right now is because you are somehow resisting their physical manifestation, by offering negative thoughts and emotions that are in discord with their emotional signature.

You believe that you need to work really hard to get a promotion, that you need to dress up in a certain way to get a boyfriend, or that you need to save money for years to purchase your ideal house. These negative beliefs create emotions that are in discord with the emotional signature of your desires, preventing their physical manifestation. As a result, all your desires remain locked in your vibrational safe, until you find their emotional signature and practise it consistently, so that they can manifest in your life.

The three steps to manifestation

There are three steps in the manifestation process:

1. **Ask:** You do this every day with every experience you have; and, as a result, you set forth instinctive and intentional desires.

2. **Receive:** As soon as you set forth a desire, the Universe instantly grants it to you and stores it in your vibrational safe.

3. **Align:** This last step is the most important, for it requires your *deliberate* attention. In order to access the contents of your vibrational safe and allow them to manifest in your life in physical form, you need to consistently practise the emotional signature of your desires.

Unlocking your vibrational safe

As I mentioned earlier, the key to manifesting your desires in physical form is to consistently practise their emotional signature – that is, the emotion you would feel had you already owned them. The process I'm about to outline allows you to practise the emotional signature of all your desires at once, so that you unlock the door to your safe and allow all of them to flow into your life at the perfect time.

The key to this process is a simple nine-letter word: *Happiness.*

The emotional signature of any desire you have is always a feeling of happiness for owning that desire. Practising that desire-specific emotional signature allows the physical manifestation of your desire to flow out of your vibrational safe and into your life. If, on the other hand, you practise a general feeling of happiness without a particular desire attached to it, you open the door of your vibrational safe for the totality of your desires to manifest.

That's because, while you feel the general emotion of happiness, it dominates your whole being and permeates your emotional stance towards every single desire that you have. As a result, maintaining a consistent overall level of happiness is essential to achieve a constant flow of favourable manifestations. The key word here is consistent, because an emotion you practise for a long period of time is much more powerful than your fleeting moment-to-moment emotions. (More on this in Chapter 11.)

Raising your overall level of happiness

Your overall or dominant level of happiness is the average of all the emotions you feel on a daily basis. Think of emotions as being on a scale, ranging from love and happiness all the way to fear and depression. If, on average, the happiest emotion you feel on a daily basis is hope, and your saddest one is depression, then your overall level of happiness lies in the middle of these two emotions. Raising your overall, dominant level of happiness means moving up the emotional scale, so that, for example, hope becomes your saddest emotion, and joy your happiest one.

I refer to the overall or dominant level of happiness as a general level of happiness, because it doesn't relate to specific reasons or desires. In other words, your overall level of happiness doesn't depend on something specific, but on your general perception of life. As a result, I will use the terms general, overall, and dominant levels of happiness interchangeably throughout the book.

Maintaining a constant overall, general, or dominant level of happiness is what most people strive for, but find difficult to accomplish. That's because our lives are full of upsetting circumstances, complicated relationships and unfortunate situations; and unless we have a strong and practised positive emotional state already in place, we are bound to get carried away by the drama of it all. We are exposed to so much information every day that our attention gets scattered all over the place, interfering with the way we feel, and therefore, with what we manifest.

As a result, disciplining yourself to focus your emotions in a way that feels good is going to be difficult at first, especially if you've lived your life letting the way you feel be determined by your outward circumstances.

Consequently, I've designed the following three-step process to help you raise your overall level of happiness in a gradual and sustainable way. Raising your overall level of happiness will also help you practise and assimilate the state of being of the guru, setting the basis for your spiritual transformation. I suggest that you practise this process for at least thirty days – or ideally for life – to elevate your dominant level of happiness, and keep doing so:

1. *Morning ritual*

You've probably noticed that when you start your day feeling a particular way, that emotion will dominate the general tone of the day. Therefore, starting your day in a positive way is the most basic step to raising your overall level of happiness.

When I finally awakened to the Law of Attraction and the power of my emotions to create my reality, I made it my goal to find and maintain a positive approach to life, in every respect. Having realised the important influence that starting my day in a positive way had on the way I felt, I decided to dedicate at least thirty minutes every morning to setting the tone of the day to my desired state.

Until then, my mornings were usually tense and rushed. As soon as the alarm went off, I would jump out of the bed, rush to the bathroom, put on some clothes and go to school. Breakfast was not in the picture, and you'd better not talk to me. Thinking back on my life, I now realise that the way I started my day was key in prolonging my depression.

Today, my mornings are as positive as they can get. As soon as I open my eyes I let a smile light up my face. Even if you don't mean it, when you smile your brain thinks you are happy, and lets the rest of your body know about it. I then slowly become conscious of my body and surroundings, and start appreciating the simplest things I can find. I appreciate my bed for being so comfortable and warm; the sunrays shining through my window. I appreciate my room, my clothes, my books, and furnishings – anything that comes to mind. It's important to find things that are easy to appreciate, and not some complicated relationship with a friend. Don't fall into the trap of trying to appreciate something or someone you feel unsure about. This won't provide you with the pure-positive start to the day that you seek. Instead, focus on the simple things in life, with as little ambiguity about them as possible.

Following my two- or three-minute ritual of appreciation, I slowly get out of the bed, give my body a good stretch and head to the bathroom. I've got post-its all around my bathroom mirror with positive affirmations about me and my life, so as soon as I walk in I'm instantly welcomed by something positive. I read them once or twice, and then I look at myself in the mirror and say, "I love you." When you do this, you affirm that you are worthy of love, and you demand that your day be filled with the emotion of love (more about self-love in Chapter 5).

After I'm freshened up, I go back to my bed, sit in a comfortable position, put on some nice relaxing music, and meditate for fifteen minutes. Meditation is the perfect tool for raising your vibrational frequency to a general level of happiness, because when you cease thought, your body returns to its natural state of being and its original emotion – love and happiness (more about meditation in the next chapter).

Following the meditation, I go to the kitchen and make something tasty for breakfast. I choose nutritious, organic foods that are full of life-force energy. While I enjoy my breakfast I make sure to mentally appreciate my food for providing me with vitality and well-being. Doing this infuses the food with love and appreciation, which doesn't only make the food taste better, but also transfers the appreciation to your whole body when you eat it.

Right after my breakfast, I turn on my computer and open a document I've assigned solely for positive affirmations and appreciation. I sit for two or three minutes and do some more appreciation about life and myself. I always end my affirmations with "I am open and receptive to all the good, the abundance and prosperity in the Universe," an affirmation I learned from Louise Hay. Louise suggests that doing this affirmation declares to the Universe that we are open to receive all of the positive things we have amassed in our vibrational safe.

By that moment, I'm feeling joyful and exhilarated, and I can't wait to put on something chic and stylish and start my day. It's fascinating the way a simple thirty-minute morning ritual can literally transform your attitude throughout the day. It's even more fascinating to think about the effects that this ritual will have on your attitude after you've practised it for a whole month. Things that used to irritate you will feel insignificant; the people who saddened you will magically disappear; and you will be marching through life beaming with happiness and empowerment.

Use my morning ritual as a framework on which to design your own in a way that fits into your everyday schedule and preferences. Choose at least three activities that you can add to your morning ritual, to strategically and consciously raise your overall level of happiness.

2. Evening ritual

The thoughts and emotions you take with you to sleep determine, to a great extent, the way you feel when you first wake up. For me, drifting off into sleep was often synonymous with torture. As soon as I went to bed I would replay in my mind everything bad that had happened during the day, and very often I would cry myself to sleep. This is an awful way to end your day, for it sets the tone of your dream state, and your morning, to a negative, low-vibrational one.

A more positive approach to ending your day is to create a positive evening ritual, similar to the one you've created for your mornings. You can read a book, meditate, watch something inspirational, journal about your day, draw, or just pamper yourself. The list is endless. Use your imagination to craft something that truly empowers you. It's important that both your morning and evening rituals match your personal preferences and habits, so that you feel good while doing them.

My evening ritual usually involves meditating, doing yoga, and reflecting on my day in my journal. I avoid watching negative TV shows or videos, and instead I listen to positive music or read a book. When I go to bed, I've made it a habit of appreciating myself to sleep. That means laying on my bed and going through all the joyful experiences I've had during the day, replaying them in my mind, and re-experiencing all the positive emotions.

3. Emotional magnet of attraction[3]

Specifically positive thoughts create stronger emotions, which have a greater magnetic power than generally positive thoughts and emotions. As a result, being specifically positive will create a stronger momentum of attraction, which will quicken the process of unlocking your vibrational safe.

For example, "I had a great day" is a generally positive thought that will create a generally positive emotion, such as contentment. On the other hand, "I had a great day because I really enjoyed meeting that interesting woman at the library and we had such a pleasant conversation," is a specifically positive thought that will

---

[3] Inspired by Abraham-Hicks' concept of *The Grid*.

produce a stronger positive emotion, such as excitement. Excitement is a better-feeling emotion than contentment; therefore, it has a stronger manifestational power.

Starting and ending your day in appreciation helps you set a generally positive emotional state that will fill your day with similar-feeling manifestations. This third process takes advantage of the generally positive state you've already established, and guides you to go specific with it by building an emotional magnet of attraction.

Practise this process along with your morning and evening rituals on a daily basis. Setting the tone of your day and night to happiness, along with enhancing this happiness through building an emotional magnet, is the ideal combination to help you raise your dominant level of happiness.

For this process you will need your journal:

i. Turn your journal to landscape orientation and write a positive emotion in the centre. Be creative and find emotional words that speak to your heart. Such emotions could be Fun, Joy, Happiness, Ease, Vitality, Thriving, Empowerment, or Love.

ii. Ask yourself repeatedly, "How does this emotion make me feel?" and try to find similar emotional words that help you embody it. Use this to construct a mind-map, drawing lines from the central emotional word outwards, and writing the words that come to your mind. The key point here is to try and feel each of these words in order to build a strong emotional magnet.

iii. Once you keep doing this for a moment or two, and you successfully build an emotional magnet of your chosen emotion, it will naturally <u>attract to it specific words, thoughts, memories and details about your desires, which match this emotion.</u> Write these down as they naturally come to you.

By the time you have filled in the whole page, you will discover that as you moved outwards from the centre, what you wrote was increasingly specifically positive. It is important that you don't forcefully try to find specifically positive words and thoughts, but rather let the Law of Attraction inspire them. Your only goal should be to keep yourself focused on your chosen emotion, and the Law of Attraction will afford you with the specific thoughts that match it.

For example, let's say that you've chosen "love" as your general emotional word. As you ponder on the emotion for some time, you will come up with more emotions that help you embody it. Such emotions could be ease, fulfillment, ecstasy, freedom, and exhilaration. In time, and as you activate the emotion of love within you, you may be inspired to write about the places you've been to, or movies you've seen, that you associate with the feeling of love; or you may be inspired to write down all the loving activities you'd like to do with your mate.

This gradual way of raising your specific level of happiness brings the Law of Attraction's working mechanism into light, by vividly illustrating the way that focusing on something in general eventually attracts more of the specifics of it into your life. In time, these specifics will gain so much momentum that they will go from being specific thoughts to being full-blown physical manifestations.

It is my hope that by re-discovering the Law of Attraction you will feel energised and empowered for the spiritual journey you've just begun. Raising your overall level of happiness is, in my opinion, the simplest way to leverage on the Law of Attraction; to not just manifest your everyday desires, but to manifest the necessary concepts and processes that you need to thrive in your life purpose, and awaken the guru who lies dormant inside you.

Chapter 4
YOUR DIVINE SELF

Have you ever noticed the way little babies interact with their environment and with people in general? They don't hold any grudges against their parents, they don't get depressed or angry towards life, and they certainly don't hate anything or anyone. In fact, when you observe the nature of children you will realise that they are all about love. They love their bodies, they love their world, and they love their lives. They don't complain about their looks and they don't judge themselves for making mistakes. They simply flow with the rhythm of life.

Fast-forward the lives of babies to the age of 40 years old and their lives have gone from heaven to hell. The same babies are now serious grown-ups dealing with the "hardships" of life. They work long hours in boring jobs; argue with, and gossip about, their colleagues; go behind their friends' backs to satisfy their egotism; criticise themselves for gaining some weight over the holidays; constantly whine about how unfair the government is and how the economy's ruining their life;

engage in unhealthy habits of drinking and smoking; and they rarely have time to do the things that make their hearts sing.

Take an objective look at yourself and see how you relate to the above picture. Is your present state closer to the pure-positive, innocent baby, or the stressed-out, hurting adult?

From Angels to Demons

To really understand the workings of this radical transformation you need to take a closer look to the way you have been brought up – the nature and history of the family you grew up into, the influences from your teachers, the media, the school structure, and the rules that were imposed on you by society and the government.

Because, as much free will as you have as an individual person, your early and teenage years revolved around your parents, the other adults in your life, and the societal systems you were exposed to. As a child you were dependent on the elders in your life for sustaining your physical, mental and emotional wellbeing; and as a result, your beliefs and perspectives on life were unavoidably affected by everyone and everything around you.

Your parents said, "Don't talk to strangers," emphasising that the world is evil and people are out to get you. Your teachers taught you that you need to work hard at school to get good grades, and struggle to achieve your goals. The movies, TV series, and advertisements you've been exposed to have trained you to idolise particular stereotypes; and all of a sudden you've established binaries of beautiful and ugly, smart and dumb, right and wrong. For your entire life you've been trained into fear-based beliefs about life, other people, and yourself, and you've completely forgotten that deep down, you are still that beautiful, positive little baby that's full of wonder and happiness.

Reclaiming Your Divine Self

My aim in awakening you to the above information is not to bring up blame or resentment towards your friends and family, or the way that our world is being run. Blaming others will only lead to disempowerment and victimisation, and prevent you from reclaiming your Divine Self. Instead of feeling resentful, be grateful for awakening to the truth and seeing the big picture.

Understand that the adults in your life were also victims of the system. They only taught you what they considered to be true, and their aim was to provide you with the guidance that, in their view, would help you have a better life. Your parents and teachers never wanted you to feel fearful or victimised, and their intent was only to protect you from what they considered to be a harsh and unpredictable world. You can't blame them for loving you and offering their advice, even if it came from a place of fear. Remember that everybody used to be a loving little baby, and that they were indoctrinated by the *status quo*, too. Somehow, along the path of the history of humanity, people strayed away from their natural state of love into one of worry and fear. What's done is done, and blame will lead you nowhere close to regaining your alignment to your Divine Self.

A more empowering approach is to make the conscious decision to re-discover who you really are. It's never too late or too difficult to change, as long as you have the determination and put in the effort. Re-discovering your natural way of being is one of the most important steps to self-empowerment; for only then will you understand the immensity of your creative power, and your ability to succeed in your life purpose. Reclaiming your Divine Self is realising that you were the guru all along; the only difference being that you can now consciously act on it.

Exploring Your Divine Self

Unless you experience it, it isn't real. You can read hundreds of books and articles on your true nature and still not be convinced of it. However, when you experience something, its truth is incontrovertible. You feel it with all your senses, and your entire being screams that it's true. As a result, I've designed the practical section of this chapter in a way that will help you experience your Divine Self.

Before we jump right into the process that will help you do that, it's important to explore your true nature with words first, and define it in a comprehensive way. This will provide you with a conceptual understanding of your Divine Self, so that you can experience and assimilate it in the forthcoming process.

The story of creation

Before you (and every single piece of consciousness in this universe) came into this physical body, you were non-physical Source consciousness – God, Spirit or however you want to define it. Source knew it was invincible, and that it had immense creative powers. However, being non-physical, it couldn't express its creative power in a tangible way, and therefore it couldn't grow into that which it was.

As a result, Source decided to express itself in physical form. And so, it moulded itself into physical matter. It expressed itself as suns and planets, oceans and mountains, glaciers and volcanoes, animals and humans. Planet Earth, in particular, provided a wide diversity that was perfect for facilitating the growth of consciousness that Source desired: a place with contrasting physical environments, and millions of people with different opinions, religions, ethnicities, desires and beliefs.

From your non-physical, Source standpoint, you had full awareness of the story of creation. You understood that by coming here you would expose yourself to a wide diversity of experiences, both positive and negative, that would allow you to formulate desires. Most importantly, you trusted that the Law of Attraction would bring them into manifestation, and as a result, expand consciousness.

Since the beginning of time, we have used this exact formula, either consciously or unconsciously, to become what we are today. We've gone from living in caves and feeding on raw meat to living in highly technological megacities and feeding on *haute cuisine*.

Two Definitions

As mentioned above, everything in the Universe is a physical extension of non-physical Source consciousness. But what does this mean on a personal level? And what are the fundamental qualities of that Source consciousness – your Divine Self?

Flames of the same sun: My favourite analogy, which captures our true essence perfectly, is by Neale Donald Walsch, and suggests that we are all flames of the same sun[1]. In other words, we are individual expressions, the flames; but we are all part of a single source of consciousness, the Sun. Therefore, even though we have unique physical bodies, characteristics and personalities, our core is the same, and belongs to one stream of consciousness. This is true for every single piece of consciousness in this universe, living or inanimate.

Love and light: What is that one stream of consciousness made of? Love and light. When you zoom into every single piece of consciousness in the Universe you'll find out that it's made out of vibration – which is energy – and therefore light.

What holds this light-stream of consciousness together, and defines it, is love. If you ponder on this, love is everywhere in our lives. We write books about it, make films, tell stories, and are in a constant quest to find it – in our relationships, hobbies, and careers. Everything you do is done so that you can feel the emotion of love, because deep down you know that it's what you are made of.

Degrees of alignment

The question is, to what extent are you aligned with the love that defines you? As mentioned earlier, although you were born into love, you eventually dissipated away from it as a result of societal indoctrination. With your ability to focus your consciousness in this physical world comes also your ability to navigate a whole array of emotions. The better you feel, the more aligned you are with your Divine Self; and the worse you feel, the more misaligned you are from it.

Being the guru is not necessarily about being connected to love 24/7. You are not here to be constantly loving and blissful, for you chose to be born in a world that is full of contrasting experiences, and inspires all kinds of emotions. Your quest is to gradually raise your general state of being to a more loving one so that you can be aligned to your Divine Self most of the time; and leverage on the Law of Attraction to manifest the desires that result from the negative emotions that come once in a while.

As mentioned above, the more aligned you are to the emotion of love, the closer you are to being your Divine Self. That said, feeling hatred or any form of negative emotion doesn't disconnect you completely from your Divine Self. You can never be a hundred percent disconnected from your loving core, because you are literally made out of it. Even though you are a physical being, the largest part of you is spiritual and energetic; and that energy is love and light.

Whereas there is a limit to how disconnected you can be from your Divine Self, there cannot be a limit to your degree of alignment to it. In other words, you can never be a hundred percent loving – there is always more love to be experienced. There is no boundary to the goodness and loveliness that you can feel. You can always feel better; and in doing so become more, and more, and more of your Divine Self.

A note on terms: Love and happiness have similar vibrational frequencies; therefore, by being in alignment with your loving Divine Self you automatically find happiness too, and unlock your vibrational safe. *Vice versa*, by raising your general level of happiness as suggested in Chapter 3, you concurrently align yourself to love, and your Divine Self.

Experiencing Your Divine Self

If there were a single process to help you experience your Divine Self, and therefore help you align with the emotion of love, this would be meditation. Meditation is the simple act of quieting your mind from thoughts. As mentioned in Chapter 3, thoughts create emotions. When you stop thinking, your being will automatically return to its original state, and you will feel your original emotion – love.

The following meditation process will guide you into quieting your mind enough so that you can experience your Divine Self. For maximum results, include meditation in your morning ritual, to ensure that you bring the whole of you into your daily activities:

1. **Find a quiet place and sit in a comfortable position.** You may light candles or put on meditative music if you like, to help you calm down and relax. It's important that you wear comfortable clothes and dim the lighting in the room.

2. **Close your eyes and consciously relax your body.** The most effective way to do so is by mentally relaxing your body parts one by one, starting from the top of your head and moving down to the tips of your feet. If it helps, you may want to purposely tense each body part first and then relax it, to better feel the release of tension.

3. **Focus on your breathing.** The aim is to give your mind as little to think about as possible. Your mind is made to think, so attempting to cease thought completely is not an easy thing to accomplish. Instead, concentrating on your breathing gives your mind something small and insignificant to focus on. If thoughts come up (they will!), just acknowledge them and bring your attention back to your breathing.

After the meditation, take pen and paper and jot down the question: Who am I? Having aligned yourself to your Divine Self, you have literally allowed your physical aspect to blend with the larger, spiritual part of you. Whatever you do or write from that heightened place will be imbued with the essence of your Divine Self, the essence of love.

The key to answering this question successfully is to not think while you write. Just start writing and don't allow yourself to pause. Even if what you write doesn't make sense, don't stop. Your aim is not to have good handwriting, or to spell things correctly, or to use good grammar. The aim is to allow the larger, loving aspect of you to answer this question.

I suggest that you do this exercise every day for at least one week.

In practising this exercise, you will probably notice the following:

- As the week goes on, you will discover that your answers become increasingly positive. That's because your physical self eventually gets the hang of translating the impulses of your spiritual self. Meditation will strengthen your "spiritual muscles", allowing you to achieve a greater degree of blending between your two perspectives – the physical and the spiritual – yielding clearer and more accurate definitions of your Divine Self.

- Furthermore, as you do this exercise your responses will be more detailed. This occurs for the same reason. The more you practise aligning yourself with your Divine Self through meditation, the stronger and faster your connection to it becomes. This is due to the workings of the Law of Attraction, stating that whatever you put your attention to expands. As a result, the more you practise free-writing, the more words and information you are going to attract about your Divine Self.

The merit of meditation is that it gives you a very palpable and undeniable experience of your Divine Self. As I mentioned earlier, when you experience something, you know it's true, and nothing can dissuade you from it. This is what self-empowerment is all about, and this is how you become your own spiritual teacher.

PART II
BECOME THE GURU

Having awakened to your Divine Self – you inner guru – in Part II you will learn how to become it. In the next three chapters, I will guide you through processes designed to de-programme your old, limited self, and programme in you the qualities of the guru. By the end of Part II, your mind and body will have gone through a radical transformation, as they start resembling your new, enlightened self.

Chapter 5
SELF-LOVE BOOT CAMP

Throughout my spiritual journey, I realised that every single modality I practised, and every spiritual book I read, had one thing in common: the element of self-love. The value of self-love was particularly emphasised in Louise Hay's books and audio meditations, in which she stressed that the simple act of loving yourself was the cure to all forms of emotional, mental and physical diseases[2]. I was fascinated by the simplicity of this claim, but I couldn't completely grasp how it could be true; yet I instantly knew I had hit on an important piece of knowledge that would transform my life. It wasn't until I personally experienced the power of consciously loving myself that I awakened to the truth behind Louise's statement.

Passive *vs.* Conscious Self-Love

The power of self-love lies in the understanding that when you consciously express love towards yourself, you tune your mind, body and spirit to the invincible force of love that defines you. In Chapter 4, you learned that your true nature is very similar to that of little babies – pure and unconditionally loving – but you have strayed from your Divine Self as a result of societal indoctrination. As I suggested in Chapter 4, meditation is a powerful way of quieting the thought-clutter in your mind, to align with your natural state of self-love.

Whereas meditation is a passive, indirect way of loving yourself, consciously affirming your self-love provides you with a more active and deliberate means of doing so.

The benefit of conscious self-love, as opposed to that of meditation, is the depth of alignment that conscious self-love allows you to achieve. When you consciously affirm your self-love, you come face to face with fears, concerns, and limiting beliefs which prevent you from loving yourself fully. In other words, meditation allows for a moment-to-moment alignment to your Divine Self, and conscious self-love gives you the opportunity to confront your ego's objections to loving yourself on a permanent basis: to forgive them, and let them go.

Is Self-Love the Same as Narcissism?

Many people confuse self-love with narcissism. In truth, the two are direct opposites. Narcissism comes from a place of fear, while self-love comes from a place of unconditional love. A narcissistic person has no respect or awareness of his love-liness and Divine Self, and often feels the need to make up for it by proving himself to others, as well as to himself. A person who has self-love is totally aware of his love-liness and Divine Self; and therefore the ego doesn't come into play.

A Course In Miracles makes the distinction between form and content: form being our physical body and personality, and content being our soul and love-liness.[3] Narcissists have no awareness of their content, and perceive themselves as being solely form. Their power comes from judging themselves and others, and making comparisons so they can prove that their form is worthy and better than that of others. On the other hand, self-love is about both form and content. Self-loving people don't need to compare themselves to anyone, or to judge others as less than themselves, because they know that everyone is made out of love, and is equally worthy and loveable.

In his book *Loveability*, Robert Holden suggests that self-love is simply the realisation that "I am love."[4] When you genuinely love yourself, you recognise that you are a physical extension of love. You appreciate your body for being your physical vessel in this lifetime; but you know that it doesn't define you. The only thing that defines you is love.

Love *vs.* Self-love

As Robert Holden's quote suggests, there is no essential difference between love and self-love, for self-love is just the realisation that you are love. This understanding brings up the question of what love really is.

Perhaps the easiest way of understanding what love *is* is by exploring what love *isn't*. The way I see it, love is not just a word, an emotion, or even an experience. Love is All. It is a transcendence; an eternity of bliss; a perfect understanding of Oneness. Love is communion with the Spirit that defines every one of us, and every piece of consciousness in the Universe. Love is the emotion of ease, harmony, balance, happiness, ecstasy, excitement, exhilaration, abundance, joy, fulfilment, empowerment and so much more, all together.

Even the above definitions combined are minuscule in the face of what love really is, and I don't think any language has the right words to fully capture it; yet who needs words when you can experience something? You have experienced the all-ness of love many times in your life. You were born into it, you've lived a life full of it, and you will dissolve into it when you die.

Self-Love is the Solution to Everything

Love is the most powerful force in the Universe, and self-love means becoming one with this force. Therefore, self-love is, literally, the solution to everything. In the following section I will explain how practising self-love can help you find wholeness in different aspects of your life.

Self-love and physical health

The understanding of how self-love heals lies in the interconnection between mind, body and spirit. It has long been accepted that physical conditions originate from negative thoughts and emotions. Your thoughts create your emotions, and your long-term emotions eventually manifest in physical form. For example, have you noticed that you often get a cold when you're too stressed out, or tired, or you don't get enough sleep?

From this perspective, the cure to any form of illness lies in finding its associated negative thought pattern or emotion, and changing it to something more positive. Self-love is the ultimate form of positive emotion, and in the process of consciously practising it, you are called on to confront the negative thought patterns and beliefs that prevent you from fully owning it. As the source of illness is healed, its physical extension will disappear, too.

In simple terms, your natural state of a pure-positive and unconditionally loving being affords you with perfect health, and any disease that resulted from a negative state of being has to dissipate. By recalibrating yourself back to your Divine Self through self-love, you simply allow your body to return to its rightful state of perfect health.

Self-love and your life purpose

Self-love is the key to finding, following and succeeding in your life purpose. As I mentioned in my *Discover Your Life Purpose* guide (if you haven't got it already, go to page x in the introduction to learn how to download it), when you are fully aligned to your Divine

Self you naturally gravitate towards activities, people, experiences, classes, and jobs that are directly related to your life purpose.

As already discussed, conscious self-love is the ultimate way of aligning to your Divine Self. Therefore, when you affirm your self-love, and become enmeshed in the emotion of love, you instantly become as one with your life purpose. From this authentic place, you become inspired with the action steps required to follow, and thrive in, it.

Self-love and manifesting your desires

Since conscious self-love allows for a more permanent alignment with your Divine Self, practising self-love is also a powerful way of unlocking your vibrational safe, and keeping it unlocked for all of your desires to manifest at the perfect time. This is because when you don't consciously choose positive thoughts and emotions, your manifestation power is, to a great extent, driven by subconscious limiting beliefs. As a result, for the most of your day, you manifest things by default.

Through the process of consciously loving yourself, and bringing to the surface the subconscious beliefs that hold you hostage, you can achieve a more holistic alignment to your vibrational safe. By confronting limiting beliefs you are given the opportunity to consciously replace them with empowering ones, based on what you'd like to manifest.

Self-love and relationships

Your degree of self-love determines your ability to find true love in your relationships, whether these are romantic, family ones, or friendships. Many people confuse true love with co-dependency. Co-dependency is when your self-love depends on other people's opinions about you. When you are co-dependent, you desperately need other people to love and accept you, so that you can in turn feel worthy and loveable. Moreover, your expression of love to another human being comes with the expectation of receiving back that love; and when your expectation is not met, you end up feeling hurt and betrayed.

On the other hand, true love is when your expression of love is unrelated to other people's responses. You love someone because you are made out of love, because love feels so good, and simply because love is what you do. You love and appreciate the other person for who he or she is, and you don't need that love back because you already *are* it. You can't need love when you *are* love.

In this respect, when you don't love yourself you cannot experience true love. Your lovelessness creates feelings of inadequacy and unfulfilment, and you become co-dependent on other people. Conversely, when you truly love yourself you become the presence of love, and you no longer have the need to get it from someone else. You simply bask in the feeling and knowing of your loveliness; and other people's love towards you is just an addition, and an affirmation of what you already know about yourself.

Practising Conscious Self-Love

Practising conscious self-love is a tricky business. You've spent your entire life being exposed to the opinions of others about how you should think, talk and behave; and to judgments about how smart, sociable or attractive you are. As a result, your level of self-love is inevitably shaped by all the programming you have been subjected to over the course of your life. The longer you believed and practised these limiting beliefs, the more they have become embedded into your subconscious.

Consequently, you became a victim of other people's projections, which have nothing to do with who you really are, and what you are here to do. Your entire life, your relationships, career, health, and social life, were all directed by other people's beliefs. Instead of owning your authenticity and going for your life purpose, you ended up taking the wrong classes, and going for the wrong jobs, because others said this is the only road to success.

How can you experience unconditional self-love when your self is conditioned by everyone else? You can never truly love yourself unless you strip away all the external programming, and come to terms with who *you* are, what *you* think is right and wrong, and when *you* are the one deciding about what's best for you.

Breaking out of these subconscious beliefs is difficult, but absolutely do-able. I've designed the following three-step process to help you gradually de-programme your mind from subconscious limiting beliefs, and to re-programme it with more supportive ones, so that you can practise conscious self-love fearlessly:

1. *Be willing to change*

As simple as this may sound, one of the most common setbacks in making the transition from self-judgment to self-love is fear of change. Most people don't like change, because when you get used to a certain lifestyle, however hurtful and unpleasant it is, its negativity eventually fades away into your routine. As a result, you become unable to grasp the extent to which you damage yourself, and you reach a point when self-judgment becomes an acceptable way of life.

The first step to breaking out of this numbness is by consciously being willing to change. You have to realise that nothing in your life will ever change unless you are willing to put in the effort. If you are reading this book, that means you've attracted it as a tool to help you turn your life around. It is your duty – to yourself, to God, and to the whole world – to have the courage to follow through.

Journal exercise

To affirm your willingness to change, get out your journal and write a letter to your old self. I want you to give your past self a name, so that you differentiate it from the person you are now becoming. In the letter, express your appreciation for all your old self has helped you to experience, and let him know that you are moving on. Be honest, but don't introduce any resentment. The aim is to appreciate the past, let it go, and start afresh. End your letter by declaring your willingness to change and grow.

2. *De-programme your mind*

Having declared your willingness to change and take control over your life, it is time to de-programme your mind from all the berating subconscious beliefs and ideas you've been trained to believe about yourself. This is one of the most fundamental processes in this book, as it will allow you to re-wire your mind to think in a more positive and supportive way in your journey through the book and your spiritual path in general.

As with all changes in life, doing so will come with resistance. Your ego will sabotage the process by making you feel stupid, weird or unable to follow through. Your ego will do anything to maintain its control upon you, so it's up to you to feel the fear and do it anyway.

Here are the steps in the de-programming process:

i. Take a page in your journal and divide it into two sides.

ii. Title the first side "Self-Illusions", and fill it in with all the things that the people in your life, including yourself, told you were wrong with you. Start from your childhood and go through your entire life, stating every single thing that comes up – however insignificant it may seem.

iii. Title the other side of the page "Self-Realities". Then take each of the negative beliefs you wrote on the previous list and turn it around into something positive, yet believable for you (see the example in the next section).

iv. Every day for at least thirty days, read each self-reality and try to embody the way it feels. It's important not to just skim through them, but to actually take the time to bask in the emotion each one creates. As Abraham-Hicks say, a belief is just a thought you keep thinking. The more you repeat, and feel, these self-realities, the sooner you will believe them.

Self-Realities Guidelines

To formulate effective self-realities follow these guidelines:

- **Make them both positive and believable**: For example, if the limiting belief is, "I am fat," then this would change into something like, "I am in the process of losing unnecessary weight." Changing it to, "I am slim" may introduce more negativity, as this may feel like a lie to you. Use phrases such as, "I am in the process of...," and "I am constantly improving my..." to shift the negative belief into something more believable. Use your gut feeling to decide how each self-reality feels, ensuring that no resistance is introduced.

- **Read behind the lines**: Sometimes, you will need to find the deeper reason behind a belief. For example, being overweight may be due to your inability to face your fears, so that you end up bingeing on fat and sugar. In this case, the self-reality would be something along the lines of, "I am in the process of accepting and healing my fears." Once again, use your gut instincts to judge whether you've hit the right wording or not, and adjust accordingly.

- **Avoid negative words**: It's also important to avoid using negative words. Don't empower the problem by using phrases like, "I will not..." or "I will avoid..." Instead, choose to affirm the solution with, "I am" or "I am going to..." Before you finalise a self-reality, read through it once again to ensure that none of the words you used introduce negativity. This may seem an unnecessary precaution, but words have vibration. The more positive they are the higher their vibration, and the more in alignment they are to your Divine Self.

3. Practise mirror work

Mirror work changed my life. I first found out about it in Louise Hay's book *You Can Heal Your Life*. In the book, Louise suggested that I look at myself in the mirror and say, "George, I love you." Although the idea of looking at myself in the mirror and saying anything seemed odd and childish, I decided to give the process a chance. Facing myself in the mirror, I looked into my eyes and mumbled a stifled, "I love..." and then paused in defiance. I became inexplicably overwhelmed. My whole body had revolted against the idea of loving myself and a wave of guilt surged through me, causing an implosion of uncontrollable crying.

At that moment I was struck by the power of Mirror Work, and despite my ego's resistance, I was determined to keep at it until I reached the point where mumbling would turn into declaring, and I would proudly be able to express love to myself.

How it works

When you look at yourself in the mirror and make a statement, the mirror will reflect back to you all the thoughts, fears and beliefs that defy that statement. Looking into your eyes has the power of stripping away all the ego's illusory perspectives, allowing you to see straight into your soul. When you look into your eyes, all of your masks come off and you face the truth.

For this reason, Mirror Work will probably be the hardest process for you to stick with, but it will also be the most rewarding. When I consciously expressed love to myself in the mirror, I was bombarded with all the limiting beliefs I held about myself that resisted the self-love. They were so many that my body couldn't take it, which caused me to feel overwhelmed and burst into tears.

For this reason, it's important that you practise Mirror Work in a gradual way. The three processes provided here will guide you through a shock-free approach to Mirror Work. When you are finally done with them, you will be able to look straight into your eyes, say, "I love you," and believe it with all of your heart.

Your current self-love level

Before you start with the first process, it's important to determine your current level of self-love. Knowing where you stand in relation to where you want to go will allow you to track your progress through the process.

Face yourself in the mirror and look into your eyes. Take some time basking in this state, and when you are ready say, "[Your Name], I love you;" notice how you feel, and where you feel it in your body. Try to name the emotion, and make a note of it in your journal. If you can't turn it into words, don't worry. Feeling the emotion is enough, as it still gives you a sense of how distant you are from unconditional self-love.

Shock-Free Mirror Work

Having established your current self-love level, you can now start enhancing it through the following three processes. Practise each process for at least one week before you move on to the next one. All three of the processes can be practised along with your thirty-day *mind de-programming* and *raising your overall level of happiness* practices:

i. **Practise silent self-love:** Practise silent self-love by simply looking into your eyes for five minutes every day. As I mentioned earlier, your eyes are the doorway to your soul. Therefore, by exposing yourself to your soul, to the all-loving being that lies underneath the limiting beliefs, you inadvertently heal and release these limiting beliefs. If you find yourself crying while practising silent self-love, encourage it. Unlike common belief, crying is not the creation of negativity, but rather the release of it.

ii. **Have some mirror self-talk:** Mirror self-talk involves having a five-minute conversation with yourself every day, preferably at the end of the day. Spend some time looking into the mirror and talking to yourself about your day. The purpose of this exercise is to help you develop a more intimate relationship with your Divine Self. Things become much more real when you verbalise them, because you give them value and energy. It's funny how we all think we know ourselves, yet we've never actually had a conversation with ourselves. You will be surprised how much you don't know about your own self.

iii. **Do mirror affirmations:** Having completed the previous two mirror processes, you are now in a good place to deliberately affirm your self-love. Look into your eyes and say, "[Your name], I love you." If this is still too much, soften the affirmation with, "I am willing to love you," "I like you," "I am willing to like you," or "I am willing to give you a chance." Choose the one that feels most comfortable to say while still giving some level of discomfort, to bring up unexpressed limiting beliefs. Repeat the affirmation for five minutes every day. In subsequent weeks, and as the current affirmation feels better, work yourself up to affirming "I love you," and meaning it.

While practising the above exercises you will most probably unearth limiting thoughts and beliefs that didn't come up during the *mind de-programming* exercise. Keep a note of these beliefs in your journal, and follow the same steps to transform them into self-realities.

Through the practice of consciously loving yourself you attune your entire being to the essence of your Divine Self; and in doing so you get to assimilate the essence of the guru. As the perspective and being-ness of who you are changes, so will your perspective and experience of every single aspect of your life.

Chapter 6
RADICAL FORGIVENESS

When I consciously decided to embark on a path of love and self-empowerment I realised that I held deep blame and resentment towards my family, teachers, friends, and all the people who had bullied me at school. I felt guilty for not standing up to them, and guilty for demoting myself to an outcast in a society of stereotypes. As a result of all that resentment bubbling up inside me, when something good happened in my life I would sabotage it with my ugly past. I held myself hostage in a vicious circle of victimisation that ate me up day after day.

Forgiving all those people, myself included, seemed impossible at the time. How could I forgive my classmates for berating me every time I dared to express my opinion? How could I forgive my teachers who remained passive observers when people bullied me? How could I forgive myself for being a coward and not standing up for myself? The idea of forgiveness seemed completely illogical, and I wouldn't even consider it.

It wasn't until I changed my perspective of, and attitude towards, forgiveness that I finally managed to break out of this resentful cycle. Forgiving my ghosts was like letting out a breath I hadn't known I'd been holding. I felt relieved and liberated, and I was ready to start living my life again without fear and resentment holding me back.

What Forgiveness Really Is

The piece of knowledge responsible for changing my perverse stance towards forgiveness came once again from Louise Hay's teachings. Louise's simple words made me realise that forgiveness has nothing to do with condoning other people's wrongdoings; forgiveness is simply the act of letting go of the situations that hold us back from enjoying our lives.

When you consider the nature of holding on to resentment, you'll realise that what you actually do is bring something that occurred in the past – something that has ended – into your present and future. By holding onto resentments, you literally empower a no-longer-existent past circumstance, giving it life and permission to control you. Forgiveness is the realisation of the obscenity of resentment, and your conscious decision to let it go.

Who Do I Need to Forgive?

Sometimes, the hurt and resentment you hold for people or situations can be so deep-seated that you are not consciously aware of it. In the case of traumatic circumstances, if at the time of experiencing them you weren't able to deal with them, your ego had probably hidden them from you in order to protect you. Even if you may not be able to consciously discern these experiences now, you may still have a feeling that something's not quite right – that you've got things that you need to get off your chest.

If this is the case for you, I advise that you get pen and paper and write down the question: *Who do I need to forgive?*

Something magical happens when you write a question on paper. In your desire to receive divine guidance and embark on a path to love, your ego is forced to yield, allowing your Divine Self to come to the fore. As soon as you write the question, pay attention to the first people and experiences that come to your mind. Don't judge your thoughts, and don't try to understand them. Just write. Your ego may try to sabotage what comes up with excuses, but whatever comes in your mind is true guidance and needs to be dealt with.

How to Forgive

The idea of forgiveness is appealing to most people, yet when it comes to actually doing it, they don't really know how to go about it. In my experience, I've found that reading about and pondering on the true meaning of forgiveness helped to instil its essence in me. In time, and as my understanding of true forgiveness improved, it became a state of mind that worked involuntarily to recalibrate me.

Nuggets of forgiveness

What follows are four nuggets of forgiveness I've collected in my quest to forgiveness. It is my aim that, in reading them, you will ease into the essence of forgiveness, and experience its magic:

1. Be willing to forgive

In my personal experience with forgiveness, I've discovered that the only requirement for forgiving a person or a situation is simply your willingness to do it. Forgiveness is the difference between fear and love. Since you are, literally, a physical extension of love, your willingness to forgive activates the eternal love within you, which calls forth more of it. As a result, your willingness to forgive opens you up to an infinite flow of divine support, allowing Spirit to craft a personalised path, with people-interactions, experiences, processes, and situations that will lead you to forgiveness.

To initiate the forgiveness process, consciously state your willingness – either mentally, verbally, or in written form – and be aware of incoming signs and occurrences. My decision to learn how to love myself marked my willingness to forgive. Within a year, I attracted books, people, interactions, and *aha!* moments, which helped me soften my resentment and experience forgiveness.

2. Do some research

How can you forgive someone who berated you your entire life? And, how can you let go of your classmates' nasty comments that still haunt you in your dreams?

Doing some research on their life history often helps. Louise Hay claims that we are all victims of victims; implying that our parents, teachers, everyone in our life, is also a victim of their own parents, society, and life circumstances. In truth, nobody purposely hurts anyone unless he or she also hurts inside. Coming to this realisation transforms resentment into compassion as you realise that the other person's hurtful act is really a cry for help.

Therefore, doing some research on the people you need to forgive will help your ego, and the logical part of you, ease into forgiveness. You'll soon realise that your parents mistreated you because they were also mistreated by their own parents, or because they never managed to deal with their own fears and insecurities. Giving them the benefit of the doubt has nothing to do with condoning their actions — it just gives you clarity on the reasons behind their actions.

3. You are stronger now

Forgiveness becomes so much easier when you realise how much stronger you've become as a result of negative experiences. At present, I hold no grudges towards my bullies. On the other hand, I'm deeply grateful for what they put me through, because they gave me the opportunity to grow in ways in which I can now help others going through similar situations. The only reason you are holding this book right now is because of what I went through in my life, and how I've managed to empower myself as a result.

Therefore, instead of wasting your energy pitying yourself and feeling like a victim, choose to appreciate the darkness for showing you the light. Be grateful for everything you've been through by choosing to focus on what you've learnt as a result.

4. *All forgiveness is self-forgiveness*

The Law of Attraction ensures that we always attract what matches us. In this respect, everything we go through is a direct reflection of our inner landscape. In my life, I realised that the only reason I attracted bullies was because I bullied myself. Long before I was bullied at school I criticised the way I looked. I hated my sexuality and put myself through hell trying to change it. As a result of my inner bullying, I attracted people who exacerbated what I was already doing to myself.

From this perspective, the only reason you experience anything in your life is because, at some level, you have already put yourself through that experience, either mentally, emotionally, or even physically. Although this may be hard to accept at first, there is nothing more liberating than taking charge of your life and owning your experiences. Being the guru is liberating; not because you have a bunch of spiritual tools to show off to your friends, but because you have the courage to own the whole of you, and use these tools to bring yourself home.

Three Forgiveness Processes

Although your path to forgiveness will be personal, I want to share with you three powerful forgiveness processes that worked wonders for me. Use these processes for inspiration to create your own, or even to initiate the forgiveness process if you are guided to do so:

1. *Mirror self-talk*

There are no negative experiences – just your negative perception of experiences. This perspective draws from the understanding that thoughts create emotions; and that by changing your thoughts, you change their associated emotions. Resentment is an emotion too, and you can literally think yourself out of it.

I've found that a powerful way to do so is through mirror self-talk. As mentioned in the previous chapter, looking at yourself in the mirror has the power of stripping away illusion and showing you the truth. When you look into your eyes you can't lie to yourself. You are forced to be honest and express what you truly feel. By using the nuggets of inspiration mentioned earlier, you can soothe your perception of past experiences and talk yourself into a state of forgiveness.

To practise mirror self-talk, follow these steps:

i. Face yourself in the mirror and look into your eyes. Stay in this position for a few minutes, allowing your ego to melt away, and establishing a connection with your soul.

ii. When it feels right, start talking about the person or people you wish to forgive. Be brutally honest about what happened and how you feel. Don't hold anything back.

iii. When you've got everything out, use the nuggets of inspiration to soothe your resentment and find forgiveness. See their personal hurt in their actions, acknowledge that they are also victims of society, and choose to see how you've become stronger as a result of your experience with them.

Use these three steps as guidelines. You will probably discover that, as soon as you start talking honestly to yourself, you will be guided to say everything that needs expressing. Let the momentum guide you, but encourage yourself to eventually make the transition from venting to forgiveness.

2. Forgiveness visualisation

An alternative to the mirror self-talk is incorporating self-talk in visualisation. The technique I'm going to offer here will help you assimilate the benefits of self-talk with the use of visualisation, giving you a more palpable forgiveness experience:

i. Sit in a comfortable position and close your eyes. Follow the three steps in the meditation technique I offered in Chapter 3 to get into a meditative state. When you find yourself in that relaxing, blissful state, bring all the people you wish to forgive into your awareness, standing in a circle around you.

ii. In your mind's eyes, have each one of them (including a version of yourself) sit right in front of you, one at a time. Don't feel threatened by this, for everything happens in your own mind. Be assertive and engage in an honest conversation, explaining how you felt during your negative interaction with them. Let your emotions do the talking; refrain from being offensive, but make sure that you get it all out. Your aim is to help them understand that the way they treated you hurt your feelings.

iii. After you've got all your anger out, use the nuggets of forgiveness to facilitate the forgiveness process.

iv. Having expressed everything, visualise them apologising to you for their hostility. They are genuinely sorry for their actions, and some of them may start crying or even attempt to hug you. Be compassionate and allow them to express themselves freely.

v. Finally, consciously say, "Thank you for showing me what I had to heal in me. I forgive you [for this reason] and I let you go." Be certain that the message of forgiveness was fully received by them; for energy is never lost, and communication occurs on many levels, not just in the traditional way.

vi. To end the visualisation, surround both of you in white light. White light dissolves all resentment and negativity and makes sure that the relationship will unfold in the best possible way for both of you.

3. *Journaling*

If you are not a visual person and visualisation doesn't do the job for you, then writing about forgiveness is an equally effective way to deal with resentment, and is my personal favourite. As mentioned earlier, there is power in writing things down. When you write something on paper it's no longer an illusory perspective in your mind; it becomes real. There is power in physicality because we are physical beings too.

I journal on a daily basis. Whenever I catch myself feeling less than happy, I get out my journal and start writing about my feelings. Then something wonderful happens!

It's as if the paper comes to life, and I find myself divulging stuff to my best friend. I lay it all out, and I let the pen nurture me and guide me to a place of forgiveness.

To practise forgiveness through journaling, follow these steps:

i. First, divide a page into two sides. On the one side you are free to go wild with your emotions and be as real and honest as you can. You are allowed to be angry, to feel betrayed, to hate, and seek revenge. There is nothing dangerous in expressing negative emotions, as long as you don't act on them. All an emotion needs is acknowledgement, after which its power dissipates. It's only when you suppress emotions that their power grows, and eventually manifests into destructive action.

ii. On the other side of the paper, use the nuggets of inspiration to soothe your feelings into a state of forgiveness.

All three forgiveness processes are based on the principles of *A Course In Miracles*. The course suggests that forgiveness is a miracle, and a miracle is a shift in perception from fear to love. Based on this teaching, the forgiveness formula present in all three processes involves expressing your fear, and then shifting your perspective about it to transcend it into love.

Use the concepts and processes in this chapter whenever you need to re-align with the frequency of love. Even after you've forgiven past resentments and let go of old hurts, there will come times when you feel victimised, become judgmental towards others, make mistakes, or fail at something. Any circumstance that makes you feel guilty in any way is an opportunity to forgive, for as discussed earlier, forgiveness is simply the transition from any fearful emotion towards love; and therefore, a transition towards your Divine Self – the guru within.

Chapter 7
YOUR BODY KNOWS BEST

For as long as I can remember myself, I struggled with my weight. In fact, for the most part of my childhood and teenage years I used food addictively, as a way of filling up an empty heart that longed for love, happiness and acceptance. As a result, I was usually overweight, – something that fuelled up even more bullying than I was already experiencing, keeping me trapped me in a loop of over-eating and self-loathing. In high school, even though I made the decision to lose all the extra weight, I approached the subject in the wrong way and engaged in extreme diets that involved starving myself for months. In time, I got so close to becoming anorexic that my mum had to take me to a nutritionist, who instantly put me on a weight-gain diet.

Aside from my radical and unstable approach to losing weight, I paid no attention to the kind of food I provided for myself. I was addicted to junk, processed foods like burgers, hot dogs and French fries, and I was a complete meat-eater, abstaining from all kinds of fruits, vegetables and pulses. Therefore, even though I eventually managed to keep my weight to normal standards, I did that in a very unhealthy way. As a result, I always felt weary and heavy, my energy reserves were usually very low, and I was tormented by strong headaches and fatigue that consumed my vitality, making me feel older than my age.

It wasn't until I walked the spiritual path, and got reacquainted with my inner voice, that I made a conscious attempt to improve my health and diet. As I started paying more attention to the messages my body was constantly providing me with, I finally decided to combat my addictions and make positive changes. As a result, I quit eating junk food and added more greens and vegetables to my diet. The more I listened to my body, the better I felt, and I became more energetic and alive in my personal interactions. Moreover, my mental capacities reached new levels, and I found myself being more able to concentrate and come up with unique ideas.

Eventually, as I became more aligned to my body's messages, I made the decision to quit eating meat altogether and become a vegetarian. I noticed that when I ate meat I often felt sluggish for a long period of time afterwards. I have always been a person who has striven to maximise his energy potential; and therefore, being lethargic and unproductive for a minimum of two hours after each meal was not something I was willing to endure. After giving up eating meat for good, I found my energy levels reaching heights I never even thought existed, and I became a happier, healthier and livelier person. Since meat was no longer in the menu I initially had to force myself to eat more vegetables, and in the process of doing so I ended up liking my new diet so much that I introduced greens and vegetables to all my meals.

However, even though I took massive steps to improve my health and diet, I was still not at my optimal level. I started smoking when I was 16 years old, and by the first year at university in the UK I became so addicted that I smoked a whole packet of cigarettes every day. Apart from smoking, like most students at university I started engaging in long drunken nights of partying in pubs and clubs. Now, there's nothing wrong with having a drink once in a while – but drinking a whole bottle of wine, four pints of beer and a few shots, in one night every single weekend, doesn't qualify for light drinking. Deep down I knew that I was harming myself, but the excitement of being an independent young guy in a foreign country covered up any sense of logic I had.

In my second year at university I finally committed to quitting both smoking and drinking, and even though I struggled at first, the wiser side of me won the battle, and I was done with them forever. The resulting effects on my health were astounding! Quitting smoking uncovered an entirely new version of me. In combination with all the inner work I was doing, I discovered the creativity and vitality levels I had always dreamed of. New concepts and ideas came to me plentifully; I became a much more positive person, which instantly made me more sociable and approachable to people; and my grades at university improved noticeably. I was finally free from addictions and ready to experience who I really was. Today, I am a smoking-free vegetarian, feeling alive and exuberant, always seizing the moment and living life to the full.

Food Vibration

Just as everything else on this planet is made up of energy, and hence vibration, so is also the food you eat. Natural foods like organic fruits, vegetables and grazed livestock are, like you, physical extensions of Spirit, imbued with life-force energy. On the other hand, processed and genetically modified foods are produced in a way that changes their divine identity and depletes their life-force. As a result, natural, organic foods have a higher vibrational frequency; and processed, modified foods have a lower vibrational frequency.

This understanding makes it obvious that, when you feed yourself with processed foods, you inevitably imbue your being with their low vibrational frequency. Since your mind, body and spirit are always connected to, and influenced by, each other, any change you enforce on one of them will eventually transmit to the other two. This is the reason why eating lots of junk food and an excessive amount of meat led me to feeling lethargic. I might had been poisoning my physical body, but the low vibration was being transmitted to my mental and spiritual bodies too.

Cigarettes, alcohol and other addictive substances

Cigarettes and alcohol are also made from heavily processed natural plants, and so their vibration is as low as it can get, hence the resulting clouding of consciousness that results from their consumption. When you consume them, you imbue your body with a poisonous vibration, which isn't only messing up your vibrational frequency at the moment of consumption, but stays in your body and sustains the damage for years to come.

The fact that something comes directly from the earth doesn't imply that it is safe to consume; in other words you wouldn't go around eating flowers, tree leaves and grass, as their biological structure makes them toxic to human bodies. In a similar way, certain plants and natural products like marijuana, or even caffeine, are also toxic to the human body. Yet, because the degree of harm they impose on us isn't as obvious and detrimental, many people choose to incorporate them into their lifestyle.

Doing so is disrespectful to your body, which has the ability to achieve so much higher levels of inspiration, relaxation, and aliveness than any of these substances can provide. Becoming addicted to anything closes off your body's natural mechanisms for optimum health, and you end up settling for mediocrity. When I initially gave up smoking I thought I wouldn't be able to enjoy myself in social outings; yet I was surprised to find out that as I trusted my body's ability to serve me, my reserves for fun and excitement took colossal leaps, leading me to a new favourite addiction: getting high on life!

Excessive meat

The fact that I personally chose to become a vegetarian does not imply that this is the best choice for every single person, because every body is different. Therefore, I don't suggest that you cut out eating meat altogether, unless you receive intuitive guidance to do so. I do, however, advise you to balance your diet to include both meat and vegetables.

A rule of thumb would be that the closer the food you eat is to the earth, the higher its vibrational frequency. That's because the earth is directly connected to Source, and is a natural portal of life-force energy. Although both plants and animals are connected to the earth, plants are more closely connected to it because they grow and feed on it. As a result, they benefit from the constant flow of life-force energy it emanates. On the other hand, the animals' connection to the earth is more indirect because they feed on plants. Some of them even feed on each other, so their connection to earth becomes even more distant. Imagine how distant your relationship to nature becomes when you feed on processed and genetically modified foods. As a result, the more fruits and vegetables you eat, the more life-force energy you acquire, and the more alive and vital you tend to be.

That being said, the more greens and vegetables you eat the more inspiration and intuitive guidance you are able to receive. I noticed that as I grew spiritually I required higher levels of clarity and vitality. As a result, I was gradually inspired to limit my intake of alcohol, milk, coffee, sugar, and to add even more greens to my diet. All of a sudden, foods and substances that I previously had no problem with made me feel heavy and lethargic in the same way that meat did. Pondering on this, I realised that, as I grew on my spiritual path, I was called to be increasingly more aligned to Source; and to do that I needed to provide myself with increasingly higher-vibrational foods and beverages.

In this sense, the more inspiration, vitality, and intuitive guidance you need to thrive in your life purpose, the lighter and greener your diet should be. To be the light, you have to eat in the light.

Food and the Law of Attraction

The Law of Attraction states that whatever you believe becomes true for you; and so if you believe that no matter how much junk, processed foods and substances you eat, drink or smoke, they will not harm you in any way, then they won't. This was actually the reason I prolonged my addiction to smoking, believing that I had reached a state where it couldn't affect me because I didn't believe it would. However, experience has shown me that, because most of us grew up into a society that has indoctrinated us with all kind of information about the dangers of all different foods and substances, the belief in their impairment has become so deep-seated in our consciousness that it's not easy to deal with.

Therefore, even though the Law of Attraction does not make an exception when it comes to food and addictive substances, you will probably find that it's going to take you much more energy to de-programme yourself from such deep-seated beliefs than it will to modify your dietary habits, and I hope this understanding can save you much time and energy.

How to Listen to Your Body's Messages

The key to achieving optimal health for your mind, body and spirit is, in my opinion, the ability to discern your body's messages and follow your inner guidance. Your body is a physical manifestation of Source, and so it has intelligence and consciousness of its own. As a result, it is constantly talking to you and giving you details about what it needs and how to take care of it.

The way of listening to your body's messages is by paying attention to the way you feel before, during and after you consume something. If you find that eating dairy products creates any negative kind of feeling within you, then this is a clear message that you should limit their intake, or stop eating dairy altogether. Being mindful and self-conscious is a fundamental skill to have; and once you get hold of it you're going to start trusting your instincts more.

To discern your body's messages in relation to food, do the following:

1. Keep your journal with you during the day, for an entire week. Whenever you eat something make a note of it and how it makes you feel following its consumption. If you can't pinpoint a particular emotion, just discern whether you feel better or worse than before you had it.

2. At the end of the week go through the list and determine what foods, beverages and substances made you feel more alive and vital. Would you classify them as being high- or low-vibrational foods?

3. Use your analysis to commit to quitting or decreasing your intake of the lowest-vibrational food in your list, and add more of the highest-vibrational food in your diet.

4. In time, and as you get more in tune with your ability to sense your body's messages, work your way through eliminating all foods, beverages and substances that lower your vitality levels.

In doing the above exercise, it's important to understand the difference between happiness and pleasure. Pleasure is a momentary emotion that you feel while consuming something or being involved in an activity. Happiness, on the other hand, is something you already have – it is your natural state of being. Food can give you momentary pleasure, but it can also enable or inhibit your natural state of happiness. For example, drinking alcohol may give you pleasure while you consume it, but it will eventually make you feel depleted and hung over, thus inhibiting your happiness. As a result, allow at least thirty minutes after the consumption of something before you note down and capture its emotional impact.

Another way to communicate with your body is by asking your spiritual guides to provide you with clear signs of what you need to do. Just set the intention out to the Universe, either mentally, verbally, or in written form, and you'll be amazed by the clarity of the signs your spiritual guides will provide you with, in a way that makes sense to you. You may stumble upon a book with vegetarian recipes, be handed an article about smoking, or catch a TV programme about health and nutrition. The various possible ways in which Spirit can communicate with you are endless, and in a short period of time you will be handed exact details about how you can improve your health.

Chapters 12 and 13 will provide you with more processes that will help you boost your intuition, so that you can communicate with your spiritual guides, and receive your body's messages more clearly.

Fit for Guru

I never had the best relationship with exercise. Ever since my traumatic experiences with football in primary school, I instinctively assigned sports and anything to do with fitness a violent and rough connotation that accompanied me through most of high school. The fact that I was usually the fat kid in the class also did wonders for my low self-esteem, and instead of working out harder to lose the extra weight, I ended up going to the school's psychologist, asserting that I had football-phobia. As a result, I was excused from the Physical Education class for the most part of high school.

Fortunately, with my inner transformation also came a desire to improve the physical state of my body. As a result, I decided to give fitness a chance, and so I signed myself up to a gym. The idea of becoming one of those muscular fit guys I always drooled over in magazines and at school was exhilarating. I never pictured myself as the confident kind of a guy, but since I had started feeling like it within, I wanted to look the part too.

Apart from an urge to boost my self-esteem and reinvent myself, there was also another hidden urge that called me towards fitness: a desire I couldn't explain at the time but know now to be the vibrational benefits of exercising. There was something about the act of working out that made me feel more energetic, alive, vital and empowered; and I could see and feel that even before I started doing it myself. I could sense the athletes' exuberance shooting out of their skin every time they achieved a better outcome. I cherished the aliveness and determination of my classmate footballers, and even though I was scared to do it myself, I felt the deliciousness of their experience, and wanted to taste it too.

Today, fitness is the addiction I've replaced smoking with, and I have to work out at least three times every week. If I don't I start feeling depressed and indolent, I close myself off to my friends and the world, get paranoid with insignificant things, and get grumbly and uptight with everything. In simple terms, I'm not fun to be around. As a result, I make sure to get my fitness dose every single week, and even though I no longer have the need to become the blown-up muscular type of a guy I once wished for, I aim at keeping myself in a fit, well-defined and healthy state that matches my inner self.

The vibrational benefits of exercising

By now, you are familiar with the fact that you are a physical extension of Source, so that your physical body is actually a solidified version of life-force energy, with access to infinite amounts of intelligence. When you exercise, whatever kind of exercise you engage in, your muscle fibres break to some extent, resulting in the feeling of soreness you usually get after a workout. This is a natural process that occurs so that your muscles grow up stronger and bigger, depending on the type of exercise that you do.

This kind of growth requires energy, so during your workout your body actively calls for, and draws, more life-force energy. Therefore, during exercise your body raises your vibrational frequency, boosting your connection to Spirit, and you literally become more. Every single molecule of your body transforms into a life-force magnet that attracts vitality, uplifting you on all levels. In this way, exercise is very similar to meditation, in the respect that in both practices your mind gets into a state of dissipating thought, which allows a purer connection to your higher self.

The way exercise works to draw life-force energy portrays vividly the interconnection between diet and exercise. Since food has a vibration of its own, eating quality, high-vibrational foods makes your body's job easier – to draw the life-force energy it needs while you exercise. This strengthens your ability to raise your vibrational frequency, helping you maintain your alignment to your Divine Self, and supporting the unlocking of your vibrational safe.

Your personal guru-fitness plan

As I mentioned earlier, everybody is different, so there isn't a particular form of exercise that's good for everyone. For years I pressurised myself to lift weights just because most guys my age did so, even though I had no interest or liking for it whatsoever. Recently, I made the decision to quit going to the gym or lifting weights, and to find a form of exercise that I actually enjoyed and fully resonated with. As a result, I ended up creating my own personalised fitness plan that nurtures my inner guru, and I genuinely enjoy following it.

To create your own guru-fitness plan, take out your journal and explore the kinds of exercises you enjoy, the time and place you enjoy working out, and the people you enjoy working out with. Choose the time, place, people and activities that you have the most fun with, and dedicate at least 15 minutes every day, or one hour three times a week, to physically attuning your body to your Divine Self.

Treat Your Body Like a Temple

Even though your body has an intelligence of its own and is connected to the Source part of you, it also relies on your human consciousness for its vitality and wellbeing. In other words, your body's health is a cooperative, interactive job between the whole of you. However, in your busy life you may tend to take your body for granted and to not provide it with enough love, care and pampering.

Eventually, your hectic routine becomes such a dominant aspect of your life that you end up wasting all your energy in completing one more chore and satisfying one more person, and your personal wellbeing comes last. As a result, you reach a point where you are diagnosed with chronic fatigue, insomnia, and depression; and all of a sudden you realise that you've got wrinkles all over your face, your skin is getting saggy, and you look older than your age.

It is true that beauty comes from within, but taking care of your exterior will fill your heart with love and self-appreciation that will have a palpable effect on your inner beauty, and then you will be able to experience what this proverb really means. Taking care of your physical body is fundamental in maintaining both inner and outer wellbeing, and supporting your alignment to your Divine Self.

Pampering ritual

Whether you are an introvert or an extrovert, it is always important that you spend time by yourself, to provide your body with the necessary love and care that it needs. No matter how tight your schedule is you can always find time to yourself, if you decide to do so. In my last year of high school I had to study for four A-levels, I was intensely involved in my school's music scene, I did my grade seven in classical guitar and singing, and I maintained an active social life. People were always in awe of my ability to be so efficient in everything I did, and my answer was always the same: if you organise your time you can do it all.

Follow these steps to design your personal pampering ritual:

1. Whether it is ten minutes every night or an hour per week, consciously decide on a time-segment to dedicate to yourself. Plan ahead so that you don't get distracted with other things, and make sure nobody interrupts you. This is a time for you and only you.

2. There are endless ways you can spend this time alone. You may give yourself a foot massage, burn some incense, take a bath or go for a swim, get a professional spa treatment, lotion up your body, get a pedicure or manicure, exfoliate your skin, watch the sunset, take a walk in the park, have some herbal tea; the possibilities are endless. No matter what you decide to do it is important that you do it with care, and that you genuinely feel love for your physical body while doing it.

Alternatively, an easy way to incorporate pampering into your life in short daily segments is by taking care of your face. Even if you cannot afford the expensive-brand cosmetics out there, there are affordable natural cosmetics that are as efficient as any expensive brand, and are my personal favourites. Male or female, gay or straight, you can add some pampering to your life by taking five minutes in the morning and five minutes at night to provide your face with some love. A good facial exfoliator, moisturising cream and eye moisturiser is all that you need to give your face a young and healthy glow, as a physical expression of your self-love.

Body Appreciation

Loving and appreciating your body for being the physical platform for your soul in this lifetime is of utmost importance, to keep you healthy inside-out. If you haven't appreciated your body enough during Chapter 5, it is time to get the love flowing. In my personal experience with boosting self-love, I came up with easy ways to spark appreciation into my life; ways that don't take too much time but are extremely effective in increasing body-love. My favourite of these processes is saying something positive about my body every time I see myself in the mirror. Many people loathe their bodies and criticise themselves constantly by complaining that they are too fat, or that they don't look like the stereotypes our society promotes, without realising the detrimental effect that criticism has on their self-worth.

Cease the criticism and start amplifying the positive aspects of your body, so that they are the ones dominating your thoughts. If you do that consistently, all your supposed flaws will fade away and blend in with your inner beauty. When it comes to losing my extra weight I found that it was much easier to keep focused on my diet when I kept a wave of body-love and appreciation active within me. It was hard at first, but when I made my body's positive aspects the dominant ones in my mind, I was instantly filled with love and incentive that allowed the extra weight to melt away effortlessly.

If it feels good, you can even incorporate body appreciation into your pampering ritual. Just sit yourself in front of a mirror and talk to your body, complimenting it and appreciating it for all it has done for you so far. Thank your body for giving you the ability to walk through this beautiful world, and for providing you with senses that allow you to experience the magnificence of the planet. Appreciate your body for working of its own accord and involuntarily taking care of itself, and for the infinite intelligence that flows through it and provides you with health and comfort; and feel gratitude for your internal organs that work in perfect alignment with each other to pump out the toxins and maintain your health. Express all the love and appreciation that you can, as much as you can, and your body will reward you with even more vitality and alignment.

This chapter marks the completion of the second part, and your becoming of the guru. In this part you've gone through a mind-body-spirit transformation, by de-programming old, limiting beliefs and resentments, and planting new, empowering ones. In this chapter, you've focused on re-wiring your perception towards food, exercise, and pampering, to tune your physical body to your Divine Self.

PART III
SECURE THE GURU

Negativity in people, in experiences, and in your own house, is your biggest obstacle to retaining your newfound guru mindset. To prevent you from relapsing into your old habits and lifestyle, in Part III I will teach you how to deal with negativity in each of these three areas. By the end of this part, you will be equipped with a practical, spiritual toolbox which you can apply to any form of negativity, to secure the new you.

Chapter 8
DEALING WITH NEGATIVE EXPERIENCES

The Vicious Circle of Negativity

In Chapter 3 you learned that a thought creates an emotion, and that emotions activate the manifestation process. In this respect, when you go through a negative experience you naturally introduce negative thoughts, which in turn produce an associated negative emotion. As you stay in that negative state for a while, the Law of Attraction makes sure you attract more people, circumstances and experiences that match its negativity.

These negative manifestations create even more negative thoughts and emotions, which attract even more experiences to match them. In time, this pattern of negative experiences gains momentum, and becomes so deeply entrenched in your subconscious that you accept it as a natural and acceptable consequence of life. You get used to the drama and the pain, and you take for granted that, "Life is not fair," and "Life is a struggle." As a result, you get caught up in a vicious circle of negativity that becomes impossible to escape from.

My friend Valantis, who was a student in the UK at the time of writing this chapter, usually spent his summer holidays working as a barista in a coffee shop in Cyprus. In time, he became good friends with the staff and manager. As a result, despite his personal preference, when the manager asked him to work full-time one summer he couldn't refuse. By the end of the summer, Valantis was exhausted. He always complained about being too tired, and when we went out he wasn't into it. I could sense that work was wearing him out, and I exclaimed to him, deliberately, that he had to cut back on his working hours, or simply quit. It was early September after all, and he would be going back to university in two weeks' time.

Even though he was physically and emotionally exhausted, he assured me that everything was fine. His choice of words was very interesting to me. "It's not too bad. You get used to it in time and it's fine. I'm happy like this." Right then I knew exactly what was going on. Valantis had got used to the masochism to the point that it seemed normal, even pleasant. I found it astounding how in just three months, the nitty gritty of his work routine had permeated his consciousness and distorted his perception of happiness. As far as I was concerned, Valantis was a comfort-loving, luxury-seeking, high-maintenance individual who always put his own wellbeing first.

A few days later, I received a phone call from Valantis telling me he'd had an accident at work, and they'd had to stitch his hand. Although I was really upset, I also knew that the accident was the natural culmination of all the gruelling he had put himself through in the past three months. His body couldn't take it anymore and had to put an end to it by sending him to the hospital.

Valantis' story is a perfect example of how a single seemingly negative experience becomes the starting point for a negative life. When something bad happens, you instantly start complaining about it, telling other people about it, blaming everyone else, and degrading yourself for it. As a result of your intensity of focus, the Law of Attraction has to throw more of the same into the equation. In time, you attract so much negativity that it materialises in the form of a physical, mental or emotional illness.

Momentum of attraction

As Valantis' case demonstrated, when you get into the vicious circle of negativity your sense of happiness gets numbed out, and it becomes harder to break out of it, let alone realise that you are in it. This is because of the negative momentum of attraction, as discussed in *The Teachings of Abraham*[5]. As mentioned earlier, when you practise negative thoughts and attract negative experiences, the negativity in your life gains momentum.

This momentum eventually becomes your dominant state of attraction, which you can't simply choose to pause instantly. It's like being on a roller-coaster ride. Once the force of gravity takes hold on you, there's nothing you can do to stop it. You just wait until the ride is over. The negative momentum of attraction works in a similar way. It's impossible to stop the negative momentum of experiences you created as a result of your chronic negativity. The only way of starting fresh is to wait until the momentum dissipates, so that you can start building a new one.

The purpose of the first part of this book was to help you start a new, positive momentum of attraction through your morning and evening rituals. In part two, you worked on removing the foundations of your negative momentum of attraction, by changing your limiting habits and beliefs. The purpose of this part is to help you deal with the negativity that you come across on a daily basis, so that it doesn't get a hold on your life and prolong the negative momentum. In this chapter, I will show you how to deal specifically with negative experiences, so that they don't create (or prolong) a vicious circle of negativity.

I am where I am

No matter what your present phase is on the negativity trail, you need to make peace with where you are. You are where you are, and you can't do anything about it. The guiltier you feel about it, the longer you prolong your negative state, and the harder it is to break out of it. Stop judging yourself, stop playing the *woulda, shoulda, coulda* game, and be at ease with your current state. You are not the first or the last person to find himself in this situation, so you don't need to feel bad about it.

Instead, feel empowered that you finally made the decision to take a positive approach and transform your life. The fact that you are reading this book right now means that you have already taken the first step in healing your life. You did it! You managed to slip out of the negativity trail and embark on a path towards self-empowerment.

There are no negative experiences

The most important understanding in breaking out of the trail of negativity is to realise that there are really no negative experiences; there is simply your negative perception of experiences. What differentiates us from other animal species is our ability to focus our minds. You can literally think yourself into any emotional state (and this is what allows you to practise conscious manifestation). In this respect, whatever the negative situation in your life, you have the power to completely turn it around by changing your perception of it.

Turn Obstacles Into Blessings

The following three-step process will show you how you can deal with any negative experience that you go through. Whether you've had a bad day at work, had a fight with your boyfriend, failed a class, or lost a loved one, this powerful process will help you see the blessing behind the seeming obstacle:

1. Don't take heated action

When something bad happens, your entire being becomes flooded with negative emotion. The intensity of what you feel is so powerful that if you can't consciously curb it, it takes over you completely and you act impulsively. What you are inspired to say and do from this negative standpoint has nothing to do with your Divine Self, who is rooted in pure love and happiness. Therefore, the most important step to take as soon as something negative happens is to consciously prevent yourself from acting out.

If you can, remove yourself from the situation by physically leaving the room, distracting yourself with music, or simply by withdrawing your attention from what's going on. If you can't physically or mentally leave, use your breath to soothe your emotions down. There is no right or spiritual way to do this. You simply have to remove yourself from the negativity, and keep yourself from taking irrational action.

2. Meditate

When you've calmed down, go to some place quiet and sit in meditation for at least 15 minutes. By consciously quieting your mind from thoughts, you will allow your being to recalibrate back to its natural positive state. In many cases, meditation will be enough to turn around your perception of whatever happened. When you attune yourself to your Divine Self through meditation, the higher part of you affords you with a renewed understanding of whatever happens, and all is well.

Sometimes, you may even receive specific action steps that you need to take to resolve a situation, or see it in a different way. Whatever comes to your mind during meditation is divine guidance, so keep your mind alert enough to catch any impulses that come.

3. *Shift your perspective*

In some cases, the negativity of a situation is so acute that physically distancing yourself from it, or meditating, isn't enough to dissipate the negative emotion. As a result, you have to consciously shift your perspective of it.

The following technique, inspired by *The Teachings of Abraham*, will show you how to do that effectively:

i. Take out your journal and write a short summary of the negative experience. Don't offer too much detail, to avoid augmenting the negativity.

ii. Use emotional words to express how this situation makes you feel. The aim is to become conscious of where you are emotionally, in relation to where you want to go.

iii. Consciously soften the situation by going general. (See the next section for an example.)

iv. Once you've softened the negativity into a generally positive state, consciously offer specifically positive thoughts to completely transform your perspective of it. (See the next section for an example.)

Going general

Going general means consciously making general statements, which help dissipate the specifically negative thoughts and emotions created as a result of the negative situation. The aim should be to go from being specifically negative to being generally negative, and eventually generally positive. To maximise the effects of this process, write up these statements in your journal.

The following are examples of the kind of general statements you can apply. Use them as they are, or as a guideline to create your own. What's important is paying attention to the way you feel while writing them. If they help you find relief and feel better, you are on the right path:

- This too shall pass.

- There is always a blessing behind an obstacle.

- I've been though similar situations in the past and everything worked out pretty well.

- Nothing really bad happened – I'm still alive.

- Everybody goes through negative situations. This is part of life.

- All will eventually be well.

These statements are general enough that can be applied to any negative situation you experience, to soothe the negativity and pacify your perception of it. After you've practised this general state of thinking for a few minutes, and experienced a shift in perspective, you can more easily go specifically positive.

Going specific

From your generally positive state, you can easily find increasingly more specifically positive thoughts relating to your particular experience. To do so, try to find what that situation helped you understand about yourself, or other people, or life. How did it help you clarify your desire? Are you stronger as a result of it? Will you do things differently from now on? How can you help others not go through the same situation?

Use these questions as guidelines to gradually shift your perspective into a specifically positive state. As you do this for some time, you will create a positive momentum of attraction that will inspire you with more, similarly-positive thoughts. Soon after, you will find yourself appreciating the "negative" experience for everything it has taught you.

Once again, there is no right or wrong way of going about this, apart from the way the statements you write make you feel. If at any point of going specifically positive you introduce negative emotion, go back to being general. Sometimes, you may find that you are not able to go specifically positive about the situation at all. In this case, stay general for as long as it takes (it may take days), and when it feels right gradually offer more specific thoughts.

The above process is one of the most powerful techniques I've practised, as it helps me deal with anything that life throws at me. As always, when something bad happens the ego will try to empower it and stay on it for as long as it can manage. Its only opponent is your determination to make the wiser choice of dealing with it once and for all. In time, and as your present negative momentum of attraction slows down, this choice will come naturally.

The positive momentum of attraction that results from your daily spiritual practice will dominate your life experience, and the sparse negative occurrences in your life will gradually become increasingly smooth and manageable.

Chapter 9
DEALING WITH NEGATIVE PEOPLE

The Energetic Footprint

As discussed in Chapter 3, everything in the Universe is made out of vibration, and therefore, energy. This energy vibrates and emanates out of every single piece of consciousness, living or inanimate, just like a candle in the dark. This is what is usually referred to as an aura. What differentiates the human aura from everything else's aura is that the former changes according to thoughts and emotions. Positive emotions raise the vibrational frequency of your aura, and negative emotions lower it.

As you move through life and interact with different people, things, and places, your aura merges with the different auras around you, instilling them with an energetic or auric footprint. In a similar way, you are also instilled with the energetic footprints of the people and things you interact with on a daily basis. This is how you feel when someone is lying to you, or how you can spot the negative person in a group of people.

The terms Empath, Highly Sensitive Person[6], Lightworker, and Earth Angel are common in spiritual circles, all referring to the fact that people on a spiritual path are more sensitive to other people's energetic footprints. I define spirituality as the act of choosing love over fear in every situation, and keeping doing so. Drawing from this definition, being on a Spirit-ual path invites you to consciously direct your emotions towards Spirit – the emotion of love. As a result, the more you get in tune with your ability to sense and direct your own emotions, and therefore energy, the more sensitive you inevitably become to discerning the emotions and energy of everything and everyone you interact with. In other words, people on a spiritual path are more significantly affected by, and aware of, the energetic footprints of others.

Moreover, as you grow spiritually and become more attuned to your Divine Self, you vibrate mostly at the emotions of love and happiness, raising the overall vibrational frequency of your aura and energetic footprint. This means that your overall level of happiness increases, so that regardless of your emotional variations, you are generally on a happier emotional level. As a result of being a generally happier person, your threshold for negativity decreases, so that people you used to enjoy the company of now depress you. Your high-vibrating aura comes into contrast with their lower-vibrating one, and their energetic footprint becomes a virus that sucks away all your positivity.

Change is Inevitable

When you realise that being aligned to your Divine Self is the answer to thriving in your life purpose and improving every single area of your life, then you are intrinsically guided to find and maintain that alignment. In the course of my spiritual journey, I've been guided to completely re-organise my relationships, because they prevented me from maintaining my alignment. I've replaced fickle small-talk with meaningful one-on-one conversations, and I let go of negative relationships that I no longer resonated with.

Although there are simple, practical processes that you can use to protect yourself from other people's negativity, there comes a time when you grow too far apart from certain people that the effort required to protect yourself from their discordant vibrations is much more than the effort required to let them go completely. Every day is a new experience; in fact, every second is a new experience, and with every experience you change into something more and something different. At some point, you and your relationships may change in different directions, so that your auras grow away from each other and no longer resonate.

When this happens, it is only natural that you let go, so that they, and you, can go on and mingle with people who match the person you have become. There is no need for nasty break-ups, fighting, and holding on to resentment; but simply the acknowledgement of change, and appreciation for everything you have experienced together.

Reorganise Your Relationships

In the following three steps, I will guide you to reorganising your relationships in a gentle, no-drama, and resentment-free way. Releasing discordant relationships will probably be the hardest, yet most necessary, task that you need to take to complete and sustain your spiritual transformation.

Get your journal out and let's get started:

1. **Make a list of discordant relationships.** These are people whose aura is so discordant with your own aura that you experience an apparent repulsion when you interact with them. Be honest with yourself, and don't give long-term relationships the benefit of the doubt. If someone popped into your mind, they're on the list!

2. **Note the type of the relationship.** Divide these relationships into acquaintances, friends, romantic partner/s, and family members.

3. **Release these relationships.** Depending on the extent of intimacy, and the period of time the

relationship has lasted, you have to approach each one in a different way:

i. **Distance yourself from acquaintances.** In most cases, distancing yourself from acquaintances is enough to release the relationship. If you no longer resonate with these people in your time together, chances are they feel the same way. Therefore, when the level of intimacy is low and the period of time you've known each other is short, this mutual understanding is enough to end the relationship, without any misunderstandings.

ii. **Release intimate, long-term relationships assertively.** Things get more complicated when you have to deal with close friends or a romantic partner. Distancing yourself from them without an explanation is bound to create hurtful feelings and resentment. In this case, you have to be direct and assertive. Being assertive means stating your truth in a loving and kind way, while respecting the other person's emotions. Do this by arranging a one-on-one meeting with them, either in-person, on telephone, or online. Rather than attack them by stating how negative they are, and listing all the things they've done wrong, concentrate on explaining how you have changed as a person. Always end the conversation by appreciating everything you've experienced and gained as a result of your relationship with them.

iii. **See family relationships as assignments.** With regards to family members, it is not advisable, and may not be feasible, to release them from your life completely. I strongly believe that we chose our family before we incarnated into this lifetime, in order to learn and grow together. Instead of letting them go, approach negative family members as an assignment, to learn how to love them, and be happy, unconditionally. Of course, this doesn't apply to cases where the negativity extends to emotional or physical abuse, where the relationship has to end.

For a more comprehensive guide to releasing relationships assertively, read *Assertiveness for Earth Angels*[7] by Doreen Virtue.

Relationships are eternal

However assertively and lovingly you release discordant relationships, there is usually a tendency of holding at least some level of guilt and resentment. Being a sensitive human being, you have the need to be on good terms with everyone, and you dislike having to distance yourself from people. Understanding the energetic mechanism that governs relationships, as discussed earlier, will help you deal with such emotions to a great extent.

What will help you eradicate that guilt and resentment completely is the liberating understanding that all relationships are eternal. Remember that we are all interconnected in a single, energetic web of consciousness; and this connection can never be broken. By releasing discordant relationships, what you release is other people's egos, and not their higher, Divine Selves. Their Divine Self has an eternal relationship with your Divine Self, because they are made out of the same loving core.

Dealing With Static Negativity

However many changes you are inspired to make in your relationships, you will never be able to rid your life of negative people completely. Although you can deal with close relationships by using the process above, you can't censor, or control, the everyday people you interact with on a daily basis. In this respect, there will always be a static degree of people-negativity in your life.

The following three processes are specifically designed to help you protect yourself from this static negativity, so that it doesn't mess with your alignment:

1. *Negativity is really diversity*

In truth, what you perceive as negativity is really diversity, upon which our planet is based. As discussed in the story of creation in Chapter 4, the diversity of our world is a necessary component in coming up with desires, which help you and the entirety of human consciousness grow and expand.

Concurrently, although your perceived negativity helps you formulate desires, the only way of manifesting these desires is if you manage to become a match for the emotional signature of their manifestation. In Albert Einstein's infamous words, "No problem can be solved from the same level of consciousness that created it." Therefore, once you've experienced negativity and formulated a desire for its improvement, you need to align yourself to that desire to experience its manifestation.

The purpose of protecting yourself from static negativity is not to be negativity-free 24/7 – this is not possible, or desirable. The aim is to consciously sustain your alignment to your Divine Self *most* of the time, so that all the desires you've amassed in your vibrational safe can manifest in a physical way. Seeing, and accepting, static negativity as a natural and beneficial part of life is the most important step towards protecting yourself from it. This understanding allows you to use static negativity, instead of letting it use *you*.

Although the negativity of your close relationships is also diversity, the level of intimacy in these relationships can be detrimental to your alignment, and prevent you from maintaining it most of the time – hence the need to release them.

2. *Psychic shielding*

In my early years of studying and experimenting with different metaphysical concepts, I came across a technique that promised to protect me from static negativity without having to sacrifice my sociability. Although I did recognise that I could easily be swept into static negativity, I wanted to embrace the diversity that it provided, and use it without sacrificing my alignment.

This psychic shielding technique urged me to create a high-vibrational energetic shield around my aura, to prevent negativity from penetrating my mental, emotional and physical bodies. This involved using the power of intention to assign white light to the unconditionally loving and eternally happy qualities of my Divine Self, and to infuse my aura with it. By enveloping myself with it, I could experience other people in all their diversity; but instead of getting dragged into it, I was inspired to channel it in a positive way, to formulate new perspectives and desires.

To practise psychic shielding, follow these steps:

i. Get into a meditative state by using the meditation technique described in Chapter 4.

ii. Visualise a white-energy, spiraling funnel extending upwards from the top of your head. This funnel extends out from your crown chakra, an energy point through which you constantly receive life-force energy.

iii. Visualise a bright, sparkling white light coming from above and seeping into the spiraling funnel, through your head and into your body. This white light is pure-loving, positive energy, and has the ability to repel all negativity.

iv. Allow this soothing white light to fill your body and expand outwards into your aura, so that it covers you completely in a white-energy ball of light. Affirm that this protective shield will stay with you for the rest of the day and protect you from all negativity.

I suggest that you shield yourself at the beginning of every day, to ensure protection against the people you interact with.

3. *Mental armour of positivity*

When you know you are about to attend an event, or put yourself through an experience with enhanced static negativity, the psychic shielding process may not be enough to protect you. You will, therefore, have to strengthen it with a mental armour of positivity. This means talking yourself into a state of love and happiness; and therefore, raising your vibrational frequency, to such an extent that your positive aura dominates the environment. When you do this successfully, you will not simply be immune to static negativity, but you will be able to eradicate other people's negativity completely, and drag them into your positive haven.

Before you set out for your event or experience, find some place alone and do one or more of the following exercises:

i. Mentally build an emotional magnet of attraction, as discussed in Chapter 3, by concentrating on a positive emotional word until you gather up enough positive momentum to ensure your positive dominance.

ii. Replay in your mind a time in your life when you felt empowered and invincible, until you embody that same emotion. Whenever you find yourself getting dragged into other people's negativity during your time together, replay this memory in your mind to maintain the feeling.

iii. Play out in your mind how you would like the meeting to go, and imbue that visualisation with a positive emotion. To do this, close your eyes and visualise the ideal conversation pattern and feeling that you would like to be dominant in the meeting, despite the other people's negativity. A positive person has a much stronger manifestation power than a negative person, and so by visualising the meeting in your mind, you actually create how you would like the meeting to feel and unfold.

Dealing with Acute Static Negativity

Over the course of writing this book, I completed my Bachelor's degree in Geography in Bristol and moved to London, to attend Imperial College for an M.Sc. in Management. To be completely honest with you, even though I was excited to attend one of the best universities in the world to do something I was passionate about, I dreaded moving to London.

Being a *Highly Sensitive Person*, I pay meticulous attention to how my surrounding environment and the people I interact with affect my alignment, ensuring that the place I live in respects my sensitivities and nurtures my sense of wellbeing. Bristol is not so much different from my home town of Nicosia. Although a much bigger city, it is homely and friendly, to a large extent. You get to smile at people in the street, thank the bus driver after a ride home, and have a first-name relationship with the cashiers in cafés and supermarkets. Don't get me wrong – life in Bristol is more chaotic than in Nicosia, but it's nothing compared to London's hectic jungle of tube lines, traffic jams, and the unbearable noise pollution.

When I finally moved to my new London flat on July 11th 2013, I decided to take a positive approach and try to adjust to the new environment. It soon became patently obvious that the psychic shielding and mental armour of positivity techniques I had been using thus far were powerless in the face of the ocean of people I was surrounded by every day.

Overwhelmed by the dramatic change of circumstances, and my inability to successfully implement the two processes that had been my weapons against static negativity up until that day, I was left with no other choice than to go back to the basics.

The magic of prayer

I got on my knees and prayed for guidance. Throughout my spiritual journey I've learned that prayer and meditation are the two most important tools to apply in the face of inner turmoil, guaranteeing invaluable practical guidance. Prayer is the act of asking for help, and meditation prepares you to receive the answer. I have always been in awe of the magic of prayer, and have often wondered about the specifics behind its workings.

Observing myself during prayer, I realised that when I get on my knees to pray for help, I instinctively release all resistance and surrender all my fears to Spirit. The act of surrendering is the key, as it aligns me to my Divine Self and opens me up to an infinite amount of guidance, which becomes available during meditation. (More on prayer and surrendering in Chapter 11.)

Fortunately, the combination of praying and meditation worked their magic once again, and I was infused with two powerful processes, designed specifically for dealing with acute static negativity, such as with the one in megacities:

1. *People as noise*

In a large city like London or New York, you are frequently surrounded by hundreds of people, incessantly rushing about their daily affairs. It only took me a few days in London to realise that its fast-paced momentum was dominant enough to drag me in too. As a result, I found myself subconsciously following their lead and rushing from place to place without really wanting to. I needed to find a way to counteract their momentum and slow down, and I had to act fast. (Ironic, isn't it?)

While lounging under a tree one morning at the Westminster gardens, a green haven in the middle of the chaotic metropolis, I wished that I could somehow take the gardens with me everywhere I went in London, to constantly instil myself with the calming feeling they exuded. Of course, I couldn't physically have done so, but I could do something similar. Despite the scourging urbanisation and chaotic urban structure that define London as a city, there are green patches of trees and little gardens scattered all around.

I realised that, while out in the urban jungle, I could train my eyes to focus on those green patches of nature, instead of scanning through people walking past me and allowing myself to get dragged into their auras. Having tried that, I successfully managed to turn the people around me into noise, while focusing on beautifully-arranged tulips and verdant street corners. Although it required some hardcore shifting of perspective, I quickly managed to tune myself out of the chaos and into the peacefulness of nature.

2. People as babies

Unfortunately, life as a Londoner involves spending a considerable amount of your travelling time in underground tube stations and trains. With no sign of greenery around me to focus on, I was bound to fall back to my old habits of people-watching, judging, and inevitably becoming influenced by their negative vibrations. Thinking about how I could deal with the situation, I was reminded of Louise Hay's quote, that we all used to be "innocent little babies."

"That's it! I can visualise everyone in here as a baby," I thought in excitement while commuting back home after a long day out in the city, and I instantly gave it a try. Suddenly, the frustrated lady across from me was transformed into a sweet little girl, wearing a fluffy pink dress and making funny faces at the people around her. One by one, I indulged in the game and turned every single person around me into a two-year-old child. Five minutes later, the train carriage went from being a boring sitting-place into a fun-filled kindergarten, rampant with lively children running around and enjoying themselves.

I had done it! With nothing more than just my imagination, I had managed to shift my perception in a way that allowed me to see the Divine Self of the people surrounding me. Deep down, we are all innocent little babies who seek to play, laugh, be silly, and enjoy ourselves. However, when we let our petty human concerns get in the way, we fall out of alignment with our true nature, and disconnect from our eternal happiness. By choosing to see them for who they really are – innocent, happy and loving – not only did I protect myself from their negativity at that moment, but I completely revamped my perception of people's negativity as such, providing me with a more permanent protection against it.

Whether you live in a megacity or not, use these processes to protect yourself from acute static negativity, or use them as inspiration to create your own.

In time, and as you get a hold of the techniques I have discussed in this chapter, you will discover that dealing with people's negativity will come naturally to you. As your alignment to your Divine Self becomes stronger and stronger, you will inevitably manifest less and less static negativity until it becomes an insignificant part of your reality. With regards to reorganising your relationships, although it may be hard to do so the first time around, you will eventually become adept at recognising when you have to let people go, and you'll get the hold of doing so in a loving and gentle way.

Consciously dealing with people's negativity is a declaration to the Universe that your Divine Self is here to stay, and a step closer to maintaining your transformation into being your own guru.

Chapter 10
DEALING WITH NEGATIVITY IN THE HOUSE

Turn your attention to the different rooms in your home and notice how each one makes you feel. What you will discover is that each room has a distinctive mood attached to it, shaping your attitude as you move through the space of your house. You probably have a favourite room – one that promotes a sense of ease and relaxation, which makes you feel safe and peaceful, and which you just love spending time in; as well as a least favourite room – the one that makes you feel tense, uneasy and uptight, and which you rarely spend time in.

When you consider the aspects that you like and dislike about these two rooms, you will realise that they come down to particular physical characteristics. It could be the colours of the walls, the furniture, the paintings and other decorations, the way the room smells, the degree to which it's clean and tidy, or something that has emotional value to you – or not. All these factors point out to the fact that your house's energy has the power to affect the way you feel.

As I mentioned in the previous chapter, your aura doesn't just interfere with the people in your life, but also with the non-living things you come into contact with on a daily basis. Therefore, the colours, furniture, electrical appliances, the overall décor, even the structure of the house, all emit their own unique aura which imprints on you an energetic footprint, which you feel as an emotion. These different auras merge together to produce a unified aura that defines the general mood of your house, which affects, and can eventually define, your own mood.

Therefore, taking the time to consciously mould your house's energy is vital to upholding your alignment to your Divine Self.

House of Guru

In the course of this book you have gone through a remarkable spiritual transformation. As a result of shedding the remnants of your old self and awakening your true, loving, happy and empowered self, the overall aura you emit has completely changed. Even though you still have the same physical body and personality, energetically you are a different person.

If you've changed as a person, why would your house remain the same?

Currently, the overall design of your house, along with much of the stuff you own, resonate with a person you no longer are. Keeping things and clothing that are in discord with your dominant aura will prevent you from maintaining your alignment to your Divine Self. You emanate love and happiness, and your house emanates frustration and overwhelm. In time, and as you fail to tune your house to the new you, the spatial aura of the house will draw you right in, and you'll find yourself reverting to your old ways.

In this chapter, I will guide you towards wholly tuning your house to the new you. To begin with, I'll guide you through the processes of de-cluttering and space clearing to rid your house of old, negative and stagnant energies. After that, I'll show you how to work room-by-room to dissolve negativity and ensure that each room vibrates up to its highest potential, so that it can support you in your journey.

Out With the Old, In With the New

De-cluttering is the act of giving or throwing away items and clothes that you no longer need or use. Each piece of clothing and item in your house has its own unique aura, which imprints an energetic footprint on you. If a particular item's aura doesn't uplift or resonate with yours, then its energetic footprint acts like a virus that sucks away all your energy and keeps you stagnant in your old ways. De-cluttering allows you to remove these discordant items and create space for new, supportive ones.

As with every change in life, getting rid of anything will create a great deal of resistance. In your journey towards reclaiming your Divine Self your ego will do anything to preserve its hold over you. In the case of de-cluttering, the ego will disguise itself through your emotional attachment to items and clothes. Emotional attachment is the same as co-dependency, where your level of happiness depends on something external to yourself; in this case, clothes and personal items.

Being your own spiritual teacher calls for self-empowerment – the liberating act of freeing yourself from all forms of co-dependency, so that you are the only determining factor of your happiness. When you free yourself from co-dependency you won't need to hold on to items or clothes to be happy, for you will already be happy – and all that these physical items will do is enhance that happiness.

Shock-free de-cluttering

If you face resistance to de-cluttering your house due to your emotional attachment to items and clothes, the following steps will help you alleviate it. Instead of getting overwhelmed with the idea of de-cluttering your entire room or house, choose a closet, a drawer, or another equivalent small space in your house first, and take the following steps to de-clutter it. When you are done with it, gradually work your way up to de-cluttering all the rooms in your house:

1. **When did you last use it?** Go through each item in your chosen space and determine the last time you actually used it. If it was more than two years ago, then chances are you don't really need it anymore, and it has to go.

2. **Pay your respects.** The easiest way to release your attachment to clothes or anything is by performing a mini gratitude ritual. While holding each item in your hand, say, either mentally or verbally, "Thank you for being here for me when I needed you. I've changed now, and you are free to go." Feel free to change the wording of this affirmation as you see fit. The key is to appreciate the item for everything it's given you, acknowledge the fact that you've grown out of each other, and then let it go.

3. **Release it to its purpose.** Aim at recycling, or giving things away to charity. This way you'll know that each item will go on to serve someone who really needs it, and can benefit from it. Realise that by holding on to it and not really using it, you prevent it from following its own life purpose of being of service to someone.

Space Clearing

Whereas de-cluttering is all about getting rid of items and clothes that instil you with old and discordant energies, space clearing is about clearing away the old energies *you* have instilled in the space. If you spend a long period of time in a particular space feeling a particular negative emotion, you inevitably instil that space with that emotion. Even if, in time, you become a happier person, the old negative energy is still trapped in the aura of the space.

The following space clearing processes will guide you into using the power of your mind, through intention and visualisation, to dissolve away all negative energies from your house so that you can start instilling into it the loving and happy essence that defines you now. All these processes are incredibly simple and practical, and can be used at any time and frequency. To start with, I suggest that you try one process every day, and note in your journal how your room or house feels afterwards, as well as your general experience with it. With time, choose the ones that resonate best with you and use them every time you feel that your house needs clearing.

These processes are also excellent to use when you move into a new house, to ensure that you clear away the energy of its previous residents, so that you can add your own.

Open a window

This is the most natural way to clear your house of old, negative energies. Sunshine, wind, and anything natural is like a portal of life-force energy. Therefore, by opening a window to fresh air and sunshine you literally allow life-force energy to flow into your room, dissolve old energies, and naturally recalibrate it to a more uplifting state.

Light a candle

Space clearing is largely based on symbolism and intention, and candles are great tools to facilitate this. With their rich scent, colour and warmth, candles naturally emanate a positive aura. In combination with your intention of clearing the house of old energies, you can leverage their inherent positivity to clear your house. As you watch the candles burn, mentally visualise their positive, loving energy spreading through the house and dissolving all the negative and stuck energy that previously laid there.

Burn some incense

In a similar way to candles, incense sticks also work in accordance with your intention. In the same way that you did with candles, let the incense stick burn and fill the house with its scented smoke. As the smoke spreads around, mentally visualise it clearing away all negativity and allowing only pure, loving energies to remain in the room. You can even take the incense stick and walk around the house, allowing the smoke to spread through the entire space.

Get a plant

Like wind and sunshine, plants and flowers are also portals of life-force energy. This is why you feel so joyful and serene after a walk out in nature. Your aura blends with the purity of the surrounding vegetation and purifies you, leaving you feeling relaxed and uplifted.

Since you obviously cannot bring a whole forest inside your house, bringing plants and flowers into your space will do the trick. It's important to select plants and flowers that make your heart sing, so don't just pick the first plant you find for the sake of carrying out this process. Personally, I like having fresh flowers in my room constantly, and I make sure to pick the ones that make me feel good. Whenever I see them my lips broaden into a wide smile, and I truly feel blessed and appreciative of their presence.

Play the wind chimes

I've found that people either love or hate wind chimes. I personally like them, and have used them extensively in the past to clear my house of negative energy. Again, personal preference when choosing wind chimes is important, and you should always buy the ones that inspire a positive feeling, for it is the vibration of this feeling that clears away the negative energy. It's important that you place your wind chimes at or close to a window, and leave the window open or partially open to enable their use. In the same way that candles and incense sticks imbue the space with the vibration of their smell and colour, the wind chimes work in a similar way through sound.

Hang pictures or paintings

What better way to clear your room of the energies and memories of the past than with colourful pictures of you having fun with friends, travelling to exotic places, and enjoying yourself. Memory is a powerful tool for awakening experiences, and subsequently changing the way you feel.

Pictures and paintings exude an aura that relates to the activities, colours and emotions portrayed by them. The key point in choosing pictures and paintings is the way they make you feel, as this is directly related to the vibrational frequency of their aura. The better you feel in your interaction with them, the more effectively they will clear your house.

Dissolve Negativity Room by Room

An orange disaster

A few years ago, my brother Soteris wanted to dye the walls of his room bright orange. I immediately warned him that this wouldn't be a wise choice, since orange has strong, high-energy qualities that come into stark contrast with the relaxed and recessive functions that the bedroom is associated with. Although he conceptually understood the point I was making, he didn't really grasp the importance of the matter, so he went on and dyed all four walls of his room in a repulsive orange colour. A week went by and I would catch Soteris complaining to my mum about his recent insomnia. In time, he gradually turned into this gruffly and constantly-tense person, he got irritated with everyone and everything, and his performance at school deteriorated.

Of course, I knew exactly what the problem was, but my attempts to explain it to Soteris or my mum always ended up in awkward silences and tension. A few sleepless months later, and after my constant insistent reminders of the bad Feng Shui of the room, both my mum and Soteris agreed to change the colour of the walls to a more appropriate soft yellow. Soteris liked the new colour, and soon noticed a tremendous improvement in his concentration level and a decrease in his insomnia.

As demonstrated by the above story, each room in your house has a particular function, or set of functions, according to the way you use it on a daily basis. Designing a room with colours or items that counteract its dominant function prevents the room from serving you properly, and creates unnecessary negativity that hinders its functionality. By tuning the design of each room to its dominant functions, you prevent it from creating unnecessary negativity, and ensure that each room emanates an aura that supports its purpose. You literally help each room to help you sustain your alignment to your Divine Self.

In the following pages, I will introduce you to the dominant functions of the most common rooms in your house, as well as what you can do to support their functions. If I haven't included a room in your house, use your own intuition to figure out its dominant function and adjust its design accordingly. If you are interested in learning more about the logic and science behind spatial energy, you can find plenty of information in most Feng Shui books.

Bedroom

The bedroom is associated with the act of sleeping, engaging in romantic relationships, relaxing, and letting go. Based on these functions, you should avoid painting the walls with bright and vibrant colours, like reds and oranges. Such colours will keep you on edge and propagate feelings of stress, anxiety and irritation. The most appropriate colours for bedrooms are light earth tones, greens, and soft yellows. If you love fire colours like orange and red, translate them into soft pink and peach colours that flow better with the energy of the room. Blue colours are not recommended either, since their relation to the element of water may introduce its associated fluidity and instability to your sleep time.

When it comes to the decor of your bedroom, try to avoid abstract shapes, paintings and furniture, and settle for a more traditional style. You can still have a tasteful and trendy bedroom without having a mirror shaped like a star, or a rotating bed. Furthermore, a TV in the room may make you feel tired and prevent you from having a restful night's sleep. All electronic devices radiate electromagnetic waves – unnecessary energy that keeps you vigilant and prevents you from falling asleep easily. If you do have a TV in your room, avoid watching it before you go to sleep and make sure you cover it with a cloth every night.

The placement of furniture in your room is also something that you need to pay attention to. Sleeping is a vulnerable activity, as it requires your complete disengagement from the physical world for approximately eight hours every night. As a result, it's important that you feel as comfortable and safe as possible, before and during your sleep time.

To do so, ensure that while lying on your bed you can easily see the door/s of your room, and avoid having a window behind your bed. The two places from which someone or something can potentially intrude into your room are the door and the window. Being far away from both of them, and/or being able to see them from a lying position, will psychologically help you sleep better and feel safer.

Kitchen

The kitchen is associated with the act of creating – food, scents, feelings, sounds and social interactions. It's probably one of the liveliest rooms in the house, as lots of people walk in and out, engaging in different activities and providing themselves with the necessary life-force energy they need to go through their daily activities.

As a result, this is a more appropriate room to be creative when it comes to vibrant colours and abstract shapes. In particular, fire colours are very appropriate for kitchens since they go hand in hand with the act of cooking, and they have that lively energy to them to create an active environment. Decorating your kitchen with flowers, creative paintings, wind chimes, and colourful ornaments will add to its creative and playful nature, making your kitchen a fun place to cook and interact in.

Living room

For most people, the living room is the most interactive and utilised room in the house. Whether you use it to chill out with friends, watch TV, read a magazine or simply relax on the couch, you actively engage in an activity. Even when you use it for relaxation, you don't usually do it for the purpose of going to sleep. (If you do, you shouldn't.) As a result, feel free to be as creative and abstract as you want when it comes to the decor and colours of the room. This is the most ideal room to show off your artistic point of view, and to be as trendy as you want to be.

Since it is a place where you spend a lot of time, your living room must also be practical and comfortable. To do that, choose stable and comfortable couches, and ensure that they are bounded by a wall or plants, to ensure you feel safe and protected while seated. Being able to see the entrances to the living room from any sitting point of the room is also an important factor to consider when arranging the furniture. You want your guests and yourself to feel safe and in control of – not controlled by – the space, while engaging in any activity.

Garage

The garage is usually the most abandoned room in the house. On the one hand, the purpose of the garage is to house unwanted and unused items, hence its inherently stagnant essence. On the other hand, you wouldn't want that stagnant energy ruining the overall positive atmosphere of the whole house. Remember that your house has an aura too. It's like a living being, and if a part of it is abandoned or degraded, this decadent energy will eventually spread out to the rest of the house. You may not come face-to-face with the chaos going on in your house's garage, but you will be aware of it, and this is all that's needed to ruin the positive atmosphere of your house.

I don't suggest paying ridiculous amounts of money to decorate your garage or storage space in the same way as you would with the rest of the house. But it's imperative that you keep it clean, tidy, and add some colour to it too so that it's welcoming and pleasant, even for the brief time you spend in it.

Bathroom

The bathroom is a space where, in contrast to the kitchen, energy is lost. Although in other rooms you'd want to complement the functions of the room with symbols and colours that support them, this is not the case with the bathroom, where the aim is to prevent the loss of energy. The most effective way to counteract the depletion of life-force from the bathroom is by painting the top wall of the toilet in a bright fire-colour. This will keep the energy rising and prevent it from draining away through the drainage system. By the same logic, you'd want to keep the toilet lid closed when not in use, as well as keeping the drainage of the sink and shower shut off too.

A bright colour on the bathroom's top wall will do the trick and keep your bathroom looking vibrant and positive, but feel free to add as much playfulness and colour as you wish to the entire room. Play freely with the decoration, the curtain, and any ornaments you wish to decorate your bathroom with. Adding a rich scent to the space is also recommended, and will complement the colourful and lively atmosphere created with the décor.

In this chapter you have been introduced to a plethora of processes, to help you completely reorganise the energy of your house and transform it into a haven that your Divine Self can grow and thrive in. After trying all of the processes in this chapter, keep them in your spiritual toolkit and use them whenever you feel like you are being drawn back to your old toxic habits. In time, and as you practise living the life of the guru, your house will become an extension of your Divine Self, supporting you on your path to thriving on your life purpose.

PART IV
EMPOWER THE GURU

Being the guru means that you can leverage on the power of the Universe to achieve whatever you want, and find the answer to whatever you seek. To complete your transformation, I will now teach you advanced manifestation and intuitive skills that will empower you to be the source of wisdom for others, and for yourself.

Chapter 11

BECOME A MASTER MANIFESTOR

In Chapter 3 you were introduced to the Law of Attraction, the most powerful law in the Universe, which advocates that your thoughts and emotions create your life experience. The processes I provided in Chapter 3 were meant to help you unlock your vibrational safe by raising your overall level of happiness. These processes were thus aimed at helping you reach a state where you could manifest the totality of your desires at the perfect time, rather than focusing on manifesting specific desires.

As mentioned in Chapter 3, most manifestation processes belong to the fake-it-till-you-make-it category, leveraging on the Law of Attraction through making-believe. The reason I didn't introduce you to these kind of processes in Chapter 3 is because you need to have a high dominant level of happiness first before you can successfully venture into them.

In other words, imagine trying to make believe you are a billionaire when you've just gone bankrupt, or are attempting to embody love when you've just broken up with your boyfriend. Being able to successfully follow through these processes requires that you are healed of past hurts, have dealt with all the negativity in your life, and have managed to raise your overall level of happiness to a state where it can support such bold statements. If you have followed through the processes, and understood the concepts suggested so far in the book, you have now reached that required level of happiness, and you are ready to take your manifestation skills to the next level.

I've practised many fake-it-till-you-make-it processes, and I have come up with a particular blend of processes which I find work best. Therefore, in this chapter I will provide you with a carefully selected menu of processes that will help you work on manifesting a specific set of desires. Of course, maintaining your overall level of happiness upholds your ability to successfully follow through these processes, and for this reason you should continue practising unlocking your vibrational safe.

The Power of Focus

What differentiates humans from other forms of life on the planet is our ability to focus our consciousness on particular desires, through the act of directing our thoughts and emotions. The reason most of us don't live the life of our dreams is simply due to our inability to consciously focus our thoughts and emotions on what we want. Most of us become passive observers, moving through life by allowing our surrounding environment to guide the way we feel, rather than guiding our focus to consciously create our emotions.

Conscious manifestation requires both a consistency of focus on our desires, and the embodiment of positive emotion in relation to these desires. In Chapter 3, you learned how to focus yourself into a general level of happiness, as well as how you can amplify that level of happiness by building an emotional magnet of attraction. The processes in this chapter will guide you to take that general level of happiness and focus it on a particular desire. In other words, by the end of the chapter you will be able to feel good about your *specific* desires and all the details that come with them, which is what activates the manifestation process.

It's important to note that understanding and practising the processes I provide here once or twice is not sufficient for manifesting your desires. The key to manifestation is *consistent* focus on your desires. Therefore, if you are serious about creating the life you deserve, you should discipline yourself into a daily manifestation practice. You may initially find this a bit overwhelming, because you haven't practised your ability to consciously focus for a long period of time. In time, and as you get the knack of these processes, deliberate manifestation will become your second nature, and you'll finally become the potent creator that you came here to be.

Manifesting Specific Desires

I've found that the following two processes are the most successful fake-it-till-you-make-it processes:

1. *Focused magnet of attraction*

Drawing from the emotional magnet of attraction process I suggested in Chapter 3, this process will help you to utilise the power of focusing your emotions in relation to your specific desires. Most people attempt to talk themselves into having something from a state of negativity, which only creates more resistance to the manifestation process. As mentioned earlier, in order to go specific on a desire without feeling the absence of it, you have to raise your vibrational frequency to a generally positive state first, which can handle the specificity.

For example, if you are bankrupt you are most probably in the emotional state of fear and disempowerment, due to a considerable amount of evidence in your life affirming your unfavorable financial situation. If, from that low vibrational frequency, you attempt to trick yourself into believing that you are a billionaire, you will end up worsening your negativity since your current emotional situation will overpower the specifics of your desire. The discord between your current emotional state and your desired emotional state is vast, so you will not be able to effectively make the emotional jump to financial ease and abundance.

If, however, you work yourself into a general emotional state of ease and abundance first, then you will be able to go as specific as you would like with your desire. Therefore, in order to go specific on your desires – that is, to talk about and visualise the details of them while feeling good – you need to embody the *general* emotional state of already having your desire first, so that you won't feel negative emotion when you visualise and talk about its specifics.

The following steps will guide you into going specific about your desires effectively, by building a focused magnet of attraction:

i. Identify the desire you would like to attract in your life.

ii. Find the emotional signature of that desire, which is the emotion you would feel had you already owned it. To do this, ask yourself: What does financial freedom feel like? How does it feel to have the perfect boyfriend? How would I feel if I owned that car? Examples of emotions you might come up with are: Fun, appreciation, vitality, thriving, joy, fulfilment, worthiness, love, empowerment, passion, *etc*.

iii. Once you have found the emotional signature of your desire, build an emotional magnet by finding similar emotional words to embody that emotion. To avoid falling into the trap of going too specific too soon, in the first few minutes try to be as general as possible. Being mindful of the moment-by-moment way you feel is the best guidance you can get to discern whether what you are thinking helps you to raise your vibration or not.

iv. When you build the emotional magnet, it will instinctively attract to it increasingly specific thoughts regarding your chosen desire. Don't try to force the specific thoughts in your mind – just build the emotional magnet and the specific thoughts will be inspired.

v. Once you get the impulse to go specific, you will then be able to consciously go as detailed as you would like, for you will be vibrating at a high vibrational frequency that supports those details, and enhances the positive emotional state you have accomplished.

The rule of thumb for this process is to go general when you feel negative emotion, and allow inspiration to call you towards specificity. It is also of great importance that you approach this process in a playful way, and keep to it for as long as it is fun. Pushing yourself only comes from a place of resistance, and will hinder the manifestation process.

2. *Visualisation*

Visualisation is a process suggested by almost all Law of Attraction books, probably because when done correctly it is one of the most efficient and fastest ways to manifest a specific desire. When you visualise yourself in the possession of a desire, whether this is a physical object, a circumstance, event, or a state of being, you allow the visualised scenes or images to inspire an emotion within you – the emotional signature of that desire. The more specific and detailed you are in your visualisation, the more powerful the emotion you create is, and the more powerful your manifestational ability becomes; and thus, the faster your desire will manifest in physical form.

The reason I didn't suggest visualisation in Chapter 3 is because, as with the *focused magnet of attraction* process, in order to be able to visualise the specifics of your desires and feel good about them without already having them in your life, you have to already be in a generally positive state about your specific desires, such that it can support these specifics. If you visualise from a place of lacking, then anything you visualise will amplify that negative emotion, thereby increasing your resistance towards the desired manifestation.

The following steps will guide you through leveraging the power of visualisation successfully:

i. Carry out the first three steps of the *focused magnet of attraction* process, in order to establish a strong general emotional state with regards to your particular desire. This is the most important step, and you should avoid proceeding with the rest of the process if you are not in a positive emotional state about your desire.

ii. Sit in a comfortable position somewhere you are not going to be disturbed. Close your eyes, and mentally picture yourself already having your chosen desire. Milk that feeling of owning the desire for a few minutes, until you fully embody its emotional signature.

iii. Once you feel excited about what you are visualising, add some more detail to your visualisation, to magnify that emotion. An easy way to do this is to situate yourself in your visualised environment through your senses. Observe the space around you – what do you see? How does the atmosphere feel? What does the air smell like? Touch your manifested desire if you can. How does it feel? Listen to the sounds around you and identify where they come from. Become a part of the visualised scene with all your senses, and boost your positive feeling. Bask in this state for as long as you wish.

Fine-tuning the Manifestation Process

I've come to realise that the more effective a process is, the more difficult it is to implement; not because it is a difficult process as such, but as a result of limiting beliefs that are entrenched in our consciousness. This is the reason I have chosen to include the above two processes at the end of the book, after you've successfully dealt with limiting beliefs, and opened yourself up to your potential.

Following are the three most common limiting beliefs that people have in relation to manifesting their desires. These three beliefs are usually so deep-seated in your subconscious mind that chances are you haven't come across them in the de-programming process in Chapter 5. Shifting your perspective about them will, therefore, ease your way through mastering conscious manifestation:

1. *Lack of trust*

One of the major sources of resistance when it comes to manifesting your desires is your inability to trust that the Universe and the Law of Attraction have the ability to bring them to you. Trust is an indispensible step in the manifestation process, for however hard you try manifesting something, and however many processes you undergo, what you wish cannot come to you if you don't trust that it will. A single glimpse of doubt is enough to prevent the physical manifestation from revealing itself to you.

In my experience with the Law of Attraction, I've found that trust is a hard thing to get yourself around. This is because there is really nothing tangible about the Law of Attraction, and no matter how many people tell you about it, and how many books you read, if you don't experience it yourself then you simply can't trust it wholeheartedly.

A simple way of increasing your trust is to consciously attract something small and insignificant first, just to prove to yourself that this really works. Once you get the hold of attracting small things, like finding a parking space, or getting five consecutive green lights while driving, then step by step you'll start getting more confident in your manifestation abilities.

2. *The bigger it is, the harder it is to manifest*

Another central source of resistance when it comes to manifestation is the belief in the bigness of your desires, and therefore, the expected "big" effort that is required for their manifestation. In reality, the Law of Attraction doesn't distinguish between desires, and it has all the resources to orchestrate the right circumstances so that you can experience the full-blown manifestation of what you want, whatever that is. Whether it is a mansion or a pin, it is only your perception of the desire's size and importance that makes it more difficult, or easier, to manifest.

The reason you perceive desires in this way is because you grew up in an action-based society that's trained you in a mentality of struggling. As a result, you came to believe that if you want to go for the big money, your dream home, the perfect job, or a fulfilling relationship, you have to struggle for it; and after you've suffered sufficiently you will eventually be able to benefit from the fruits of your labour.

The mind de-programming process you practised in Chapter 5 has already got you on the right foot. Yet, years after I have done the inner work, I still catch myself struggling when it comes to manifesting my important, life-long desires. Even though I believed I had dealt with all the negative beliefs of struggling and not deserving, there were still glimpses of my indoctrinated past lingering in my subconscious, which prevented me from allowing the fullness of my desires to express physically.

Fortunately, I stumbled upon a powerful process that allowed me to shift my perception enough, to dissolve the beliefs that prevented me from going big with manifestation. I discovered this process in Rhonda Byrne's book *The Power*[8]:

i. Get a piece of paper and draw a large circle in the centre. This circle represents the difficulty of manifesting any desire in your life.

ii. Title the circle with your particular desire and draw a dot in the centre of it. The dot symbolises the amount of difficulty and effort required to attract that particular desire.

iii. Post this powerful image somewhere where you can see it every day.

Even though this may seem like a fickle process, this picture is a powerful symbol that sticks in your mind and reminds you of the true dimensions of your desires, as well as the minuscule effort that the Universe needs to bring what you want into your life.

3. Expectations

The final bit of resistance you will face when you work on manifesting your desires is the expectation of results. It is natural to expect that visualising about your desires, and building focused magnets of attraction on a daily basis will eventually result in physical manifestations. However, there's a very thin line between trusting that your desires will manifest, and obsessing about when they're going to manifest.

If you get too caught up in the when and the how, your expectation will turn into frustration and obsession, which will work against the manifestation process. To prevent this from happening, it is important that you practise the art of surrendering. As paradoxical as this may sound, surrendering your desires to God is the easiest way to let go of expectations and ease the manifestation process.

There are two ways of surrendering:

- **Total surrendering:** This involves completely releasing all conscious manifestation action towards your desires, and trusting that they will manifest in your life at the perfect time.

- **Partial surrendering:** This involves surrendering your desires and your expectation for results, while maintaining your conscious manifestation practice and using the processes discussed in this chapter.

Both surrendering choices work equally well, and it's up to you to choose the one that feels better.

It is important to note that surrendering your desires has nothing to do with not desiring them anymore. When you surrender your desires, what you really surrender is your resistance towards their manifestation. What you do surrender is the "Why isn't it coming yet?" and the "I've been doing this for ages. Where is it!?" With no resistance, and therefore no negative emotion, you maintain the pure emotional signature of your desires, and so enable their manifestation.

How to surrender

The surrendering process I'm about to share with you fits both types of surrendering, and it is the most important process I provide in this book. If there was a single process I could give you to help you manifest your everyday desires, be your own spiritual teacher and thrive in your life purpose, this would be it.

This process is the simple act of getting on your knees to pray.

Your body is your ego's most emblematic symbol. By submitting it to the ground you declare to the Universe that your ego is powerless against the manifestation process. This humbling gesture completely disarms your ego's expectations of results, and opens you up to the comforting presence of your higher self.

When you get to your knees, mentally or verbally, declare to God that you are here to be the presence of love – nothing more, and nothing less. In the time you spend on your knees, you are not your name, you are not your personality, and you have no dreams or desires. Most importantly, you realise that you have no life purpose. You are merely a channel, a tool that God can use to teach a message of love in this world. God has a life purpose that it chooses to express through you.

This state of surrendering will have miraculous results on your level of happiness. When you let go of everything, you have no resistance or negativity, because you have no desires to create negativity. You simply *are* the presence of love. At the end of this exercise you will feel elated and completely aligned to your Divine Self. This state of all-knowingness and interconnectedness is what's required to attract the necessary impulses and inspiration to guide you in the manifestation process. As a result, when you get out of prayer and resume your day, reclaiming your desires, purpose and personality, you will intuitively receive the action steps required for the manifestation of your desires, which you previously struggled to come up with.

I invite you to add the process of surrendering to your morning or evening ritual. Personally, I choose to start my day in prayer, surrendering myself to Spirit and asking it to guide me through the day – in whichever way it sees fit to fulfil my purpose.

At the Heels of Instant Manifestation

There is no limit to your happiness; therefore, there is no limit to your alignment with Source. In other words, you will never be *happiest*, for there will always be room for even more happiness, and even more alignment with your Divine Self. All of the processes I've provided for you in the two *Law of Attraction* chapters, as well as all of the processes in this book, are meant to help you increase your level of happiness so that you can become more and more of your Divine Self. You will find that as you practise these processes consistently, and as your level of happiness reaches a higher level, you'll get closer to instant manifestation – the ability to desire something and manifest it instantly, or at least in a short period of time.

The key to instant manifestation is not the moment-to-moment way you feel, but the dominant, overall way you feel on a daily basis. In other words, as your dominant level of happiness becomes stronger and consistent, your alignment to your vibrational safe will also become so. There will come a point when your alignment is so strong that you truly are the epitome of happiness. From this perspective, desiring something will come with little or no resistance at all, allowing your vibrationally manifested desires to flow straight out of your vibrational safe and manifest in your life in a physical way – instantly!

If you're interested in learning more about manifesting your desires instantly, check out my self-study programme *A Course In Instant Manifestation* at www.georgelizos.com/instant-manifestation.

You can download a free meditation from the programme by visiting www.georgelizos.com/instant-manifestation-meditation.

Manifesting your desires and life purpose is supposed to be fun! If at any point while practising the processes in this chapter you feel overwhelmed, please take a break and go and do something more enjoyable. The key to your spiritual transformation is to follow your own intuitive guidance, so that you are drawn to practise the right process at the right time. To help you do so, the next chapter is dedicated to helping you develop your intuitive abilities.

Chapter 12
PAY YOUR INTUITION FEES

In Chapter 4 you were reacquainted with your Divine Self: unconditionally loving, all-happy and empowered Source consciousness in physical form. Drawing from this definition, although you have a physical side in a three-dimensional world, you also have a spiritual side that is non-physically based. Although it may seem as if you are separated from your spiritual side, there is really no separation. In the words of Abraham-Hicks, "There is no other side; there is just a different perspective of this side." Your physical side is, literally, a materialised extension of your spiritual Godliness. As a result of your double, hybrid nature, you have the innate ability to tap into your spiritual Godliness and receive guidance and knowledge about anything and everything.

Consciously accessing this Source consciousness is one of the most liberating and empowering skills you can re-acquire. I say re-acquire instead of acquire, because you were born knowing exactly how to connect and receive guidance from Source. Apart from your senses of sight, hearing, smell, feeling and taste, you were also born with the sense of intuition, usually referred to as the sixth sense. In the same way that you can smell the beautiful scent of a fragrant flower, hear the twittering of a hummingbird, feel the warmth of the sun on your skin, and observe a majestic sunrise, you can also hear the angels nudging you to follow your heart, feel whether a car deal is favourable, smell danger when it's near, and see where your lost watch is hidden.

As you've probably realised, intuition is quite different from your other five senses, in the sense that it works in communication with them, since intuition's leading sensor, your third eye, is made of energy, and is therefore intangible. As a result of its subtle nature, you were taught that intuition doesn't really exist, and have suppressed its valuable assistance for your entire life. Instead, you were trained in the rightness and wrongness of things, basing all your choices in set rules made for you by others; and you spent your life worrying instead of leveraging on your intuition to make the right choices. Your parents, teachers, and society ensured that you ignored your gut feelings, visions and dreams, telling you they were irrational – even evil.

People have invented many terms to define people who have managed to become reacquainted with their intuition. They are sometimes called psychics, mediums, clairvoyants, sensitives, and intuitives. What I have come to realise now, however, is that using such terms to define an ability that is natural to every single person is misleading, and creates the illusion that people who use their intuition professionally possess a special power or ability over others. In truth, what these people really do is tune themselves to the frequency of their Divine Self, and allow inspiration to flow through.

The word inspiration comes from the Latin *inspirare*, which translates as "to breathe into". Accordingly, inspiration is the act of allowing Spirit to breathe into you, and imbue you with guidance. From this perspective, intuition is what enables inspiration, and it's something you have practised, unconsciously, your entire life. In this chapter, I will provide you with tools and processes that will help you develop your intuition, so that you can receive conscious inspiration to follow your life purpose.

Why Bother With Intuition?

What's the point of developing your intuition? You've grown up learning to suppress it; you've lived your whole life without knowing about it or taking the time to develop it; and your life worked just fine. Why bother now?

Before I learned about intuition, I used to be a shy, insecure young boy who believed that life is hard and cruel. For the most part of my teenage years I felt alone and helpless against my classmates and the society I grew up in. I was afraid to trust people, and life, and I depended on my parents, teachers and other adults in my life to make the right choices for me, thinking they knew better than I did. I saw the world as a chaotic, competitive, complex system of power relations, and believed the only way I would succeed was if I learned its ways and played by its rules.

Initially, this may seem an acceptable way of living your life, probably because almost everyone you know lives by this mentality. Day after day, year after year, you strove to find the formula for success, by studying the right subjects, taking the right classes, doing the right internships, and meeting the right people; all because your parents and/or society said that this was the right way to do things. The reason these rules may have initially worked for you is because of your belief in their success; because, by the Law of Attraction, whatever you believe in must be. But be honest with yourself – do these choices really resonate with your personality and life purpose? Do you even like what you do, or are you living someone else's life?

Whenever I meet Cypriot students in the UK I don't even need to ask what subject they read, because I know for certain that they all do certain degrees. This is primarily due to the fact that these are the most popular subjects in Cyprus, and because society told them that they would get them a good-paying job. When I ask them whether they enjoy their course, most of them look puzzled, as If I had insulted them in some way, since the only reason one should go to university, in their opinion, is to get a job. Enjoyment is irrelevant.

As you saw in Valantis' case, when you engage in a negative or non-pleasant activity for a long period time, you eventually get used to it, and you may even believe that you are happy. The fact that most people in your life live in exactly the same way corroborates this illusion, and you come to believe that chronic fatigue, boredom, and unhappiness are all part of life; they must be because everyone else experiences them, so why wouldn't you too?

By reawakening your natural ability of intuition, you'll discover that you have a source of love, inspiration and guidance always within you, at every moment of your life. You'll no longer have the need to live by the banal and fixed rules that society has set for you. You will discover that life is supposed to be fun, and you are supposed to do whatever you want to do, and be whoever you want to be. You will know for certain that you are not supposed to live an OK, fairly happy life. You will know that you are supposed to live a blissful, empowering, frisky, exhilarating, all-consuming life. With your intuition as guidance, you'll know how to make the right career choices, take the correct turn on the way home, and know when your ideal partner is around the corner. Your life will be magical beyond expectations.

You Have Experienced it

Although you've forgotten how to consciously use your intuition to receive guidance, you have experienced it in an unconscious way, repeatedly. Have you ever thought of a friend, and then immediately after received a call from him? Have you ever had an unexplainable urge to stray from your usual route? When you lose something, do you ever have a gut feeling, or even visions, about where it might be? Have you ever had dreams that came true?

In all of these situations, you have, unknowingly, managed to tap into the energetic web of consciousness that connects you with Source, and received information before it even manifested in physical form.

How Intuition Works

Intuition works on the basis of Oneness. As mentioned in Chapter 3, even though every single aspect of this universe – people, planets, animals, trees, mountains, rocks, and the oceans – is unique in its nature, we are all made out of the same Source energy that joins us together in an energetic web of consciousness.

In this respect, intuition is the ability to consciously tap into this web of consciousness and extract information about any and all aspects of that web. This is achieved by raising your vibrational frequency to the frequency of Source, as you've done with the *meditation*, *vibrational safe*, and *emotional magnet of attraction* processes. As you consciously tune yourself to Source, you mesh your physical and spiritual aspects, easing the communication between them.

Your intuition's language

As I've mentioned earlier, intuition works through, and in communication with, your senses of sight, hearing, taste, feeling and smell. However, the way intuition communicates with your five senses is different from the way you use your five senses alone. In other words, you won't see a future event in the way that you experience a sunrise with your physical eyes; and you won't smell danger in the same way that you smell a flower.

On the other hand, intuition works in such a way that what you experience with your five senses acts as a meaningful sign that needs to be translated. There is, therefore, a factor of interpretation involved, in the sense that when you are tuned into your Source, what you see, feel, hear, smell and taste are all symbols that you must translate into words and actions. In such a way, your sense of intuition works on the basis of your personal symbolisms, in collaboration with your five senses, to instil in you the right guidance.

For example, you may interpret the sight of a rose as the need to call your mum and see how she's doing; and when you do, discover that at the moment you called she really needed your support. In this case, your intuition worked through your sense of sight, to make you aware of the symbol of the rose, which you personally associate with your mum, urging you to give her a call.

Drawing from the above example and the collaborative way in which intuition works, we can say that your intuition expresses itself through the following six languages:

- **Clairvoyance** translates as *clear seeing,* and it involves using your sense of sight to interpret anything you see with your physical eyes and your mind's eye.

- **Clairsentience** translates as *clear feeling,* and it involves using your sense of feeling to interpret actual bodily feelings, as well as emotions. The gut feeling you usually get that prevents you from doing, or urges you to do, something is clairsentience.

- **Clairaudience** translates as *clear hearing,* and it involves using your sense of hearing to interpret anything you hear with both your physical ears, but also with your mind's ears.

- **Claircognisance** translates as *clear knowing,* and it involves interpreting any thoughts that come to your mind, as well as an unexplainable knowing that something is so.

- **Clairalience** translates as *clear smelling,* and it involves using your sense of smell to interpret anything you smell, or you think you smell.

- **Clairgustance** translates as *clear tasting,* and it involves using your sense of taste to interpret actual tastes, as well as what you think you can taste.

Although you receive intuitive guidance through all six of intuition's languages, you usually have one or two dominant ones. After years of using my intuitive abilities, I discovered that my most dominant ones are clairvoyance and claicognisance. Therefore, when I use my intuition I usually interpret visual information or see visions in my mind's eye, as well as receive mental downloads that help me know something instantly, without the need to interpret a sign.

Finding your dominant intuition languages takes time and practice. The more you practise giving intuitive readings to others and yourself, the more apparent it will be. To help you get started, practise the meditation and practical exercises in the following sections. They will show you how to test your intuition's languages, and get an initial glimpse of your dominant one.

Awakening Your Intuition

I believe that we choose our gifts and talents. When I was younger people told me that I had a bad singing voice (and they were probably true). However, I was determined to improve, because singing was one of my greatest passions. Therefore, I took classes, signed up to choirs, and worked my way up to winning singing competitions and playing in musicals. Talent is simply the ability to align yourself to the infinite consciousness of which you are part of, and to channel the knowledge required to learn a desired skill. From this perspective, you already have the talent of intuition, so trust that you'll be good at it.

The following two processes will help you awaken your intuition, so that you can start having a more conscious experience with it:

1. *Chakra clearing*

Chakras are energy portals in your body that act as mediums of communication between your physical and spiritual sides. Therefore, they determine your degree of blendedness, and communication with Spirit. In reality, every single point in your body is an energy portal of Spirit, since you are not separated from it, but are an extension of it. However, in time, people identified seven leading energy portals along with their characteristics and associations.

I will not get into too much detail about the seven chakras and their attributes, but instead I will focus on their connection with your intuition, and how you can use them to strengthen your intuitive abilities. Each chakra relates to a certain colour, body organs, and other personality characteristics. As mentioned earlier, the chakra directly related to your intuition is the third-eye chakra, which is found in the centre of your head right between your eyebrows. Just as your ears help you listen, and your eyes help you see, your third-eye chakra is your intuition's sensor, and it's important to keep it energised and cleansed to facilitate effective intuitive communication. In the same way that you wear glasses or contact lenses when you have a problem with your physical eyes, you also need to tend to any issues that come up with your third-eye chakra.

Your third eye is the primary powerhouse of your intuition; but, as stated, your intuition works through, and in communication with, your other senses, which are governed by different chakras. Accordingly, there is an energetic interconnection between all your chakras, and they all work collectively to facilitate your communication with Source. For example, if your main intuition language is clairsentience, and its associated chakra, the sacral one, is blocked, then your intuition will be weakened and you won't be able to receive clear information. Clearing all your chakras is, thus, important for maximising the potential of your communication with Source, and allow a more organic and natural intuitive communication.

The following are the most common associations between the six intuition languages and your chakras:

- Clairaudience: Throat chakra

- Clairsentience: Sacral chakra

- Clairvoyance: Third-eye chakra

- Claircognisance: Crown chakra

- Clairgustance: Throat chakra

- Clairalience: Throat chakra

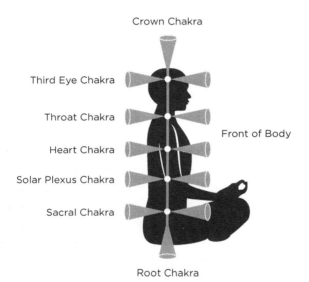

Chakra-clearing technique

To clear your chakras, follow these steps:

i. Get into a meditative state.

ii. Imagine being surrounded by white light. This is pure-positive, life-force energy: an extension of your Divine Self.

iii. Starting with your root chakra and moving up through all your chakras, breathe the white light in through the back vortex of each chakra, and breathe it out through the front vortex. (Note that the root and crown chakras only have one vortex.) See the white light dissolving all impurities and toxic energy from your chakras, leaving them vibrant and healthy.

iv. Once you clean up all your chakras, breathe in and out through all of them simultaneously a couple of times, to harmonise and energise your entire body.

Chakra clearing is one of the most important ways of preparing your entire being for intuitive communication, as it readies your senses for receiving and interpreting intuitive guidance. I suggest that you clear your chakras at least three times a week. With practice, chakra clearing will become second nature, and you'll be able to go through the entire process in no more than five minutes.

2. Meditation

The benefits of meditation are endless, but when it comes to intuition, meditation has three basic qualities:

- Firstly, meditation facilitates the blending of your physical and spiritual aspects. As you pause thinking, you allow your vibrational frequency to rise up to your original emotions of love and happiness. This allows you to match the energy of your physical body to the energy of the Spirit within you, allowing their communication.

- Meditation gives you a first-hand experience of the subtle way through which intuition works. As you establish a communion between your physical and spiritual aspects through meditation, you will naturally start receiving intuitive impulses and signs.

- This meditative state is also where you get to discover what your dominant intuition languages are. As intuitive guidance flows through, pay attention to how you receive the information. Do you see images, hear sounds, feel, smell, or taste things, or do you just *know* something with no logical explanation?

If you've been practising meditation throughout this book, then you'll have already awakened your intuitive abilities to a great extent. By understanding how meditation relates with intuition, you can now start using meditation consciously, to explore and expand its working.

Using Your Intuition

Chakra clearing and meditation are the two most important methods of awakening your intuitive abilities. Integrating these two processes in your daily or weekly spiritual practice will prepare you for receiving intuitive guidance, both consciously and unconsciously.

In this section, I will provide you with two fun exercises that you can use to practise your intuitive skills. In these exercises I'm going to ask you to guess different kinds of information by using your intuition. The concern most people have with regard to these exercises, and to most intuition processes, is how to differentiate between intuitive guidance and ego guidance. In other words, how can you be certain that you are not just making things up?

Intuition or illusion?

The main difference between intuitive and ego guidance is their timing. Intuitive messages always come as quick, spontaneous sensory perceptions that have no logical explanation. However, as soon as they come, the ego jumps in to question their validity and authenticity. This creates confusion, and you start doubting the messages, wondering whether you are making things up.

On the other hand, when guidance is intuitive you never doubt it. Intuition always comes out of your alignment with your Divine Self, and alignment equals love and happiness – emotions that have nothing to do with doubt and disbelief. Therefore, when you receive intuitive guidance you never wonder whether it's true or not, because you know it is. In fact, when it's intuition, you've already followed it!

The easiest way of overcoming the ego's sabotage is to prevent it from happening in the first place. You do this by going with the first thing that comes to your mind. Taking time to think about, or analyse the information gives your ego the time to formulate doubts and create disbelief. I always tell people, "Don't think, just talk," as this is the easiest way to prevent the ego from interrupting the intuitive process with its illusory perspectives.

...

With this distinction in mind, use the following two processes for as long as it's fun, to practise and develop your intuitive abilities. In doing so, pay attention to what intuition language you are using to receive guidance:

1. *Colour guessing*

This colour-guessing game is an easy and fun way to start using your intuition consciously, and to track the progress of your intuitive abilities. To make it more fun and effective, I suggest that you play this game with friends or family, and practise it for at least a week before moving on to the second process:

i. Get five pieces of paper and paint a different colour on each one. I would go with basic colours like blue, green, yellow, red and black first, and as you get better you can add some more tricky ones like purple and pink. It's important that you draw the actual colours on the paper instead of writing the name of the colour, since it's easier to intuitively pick up a colour instead of reading an actual word.

ii. Fold the pieces of paper, and either give them to a friend to shuffle, or do it yourself.

iii. Pick a random piece of paper and "guess" what the colour is by asking the question. Don't get disappointed if your first few tries are unfortunate, and be playful with it. You might want to keep track of the successes and failures of your guesses, so that you can track your progress.

2. *Asking a question*

Asking a question while in a meditative state is the most basic process of consciously leveraging on your intuition. The aim of this technique is not to train you in mediumship or psychic readings (this is the topic of the next chapter), but to provide you with the foundation upon which these are based:

i. Get into a meditative state.

ii. Become aware of your body and your surroundings by noticing the way you feel. Are some parts of your body warmer or colder than others? Feel the weight of your body on the chair or bed. Listen – what can you hear? What can you not hear? What can you taste or smell? Be mindful of the thoughts that come to your mind. Being self-aware in this way brings your attention to the present moment and awakens your intuition languages, so that you can best receive guidance when the information flows through.

iii. Ask a question you need guidance on, and pause, waiting for the information to flow through. Whatever happens from this point forwards, whatever you see, hear, smell, taste, feel, or know, or you think you did, is intuitive guidance.

There you have it. In a few pages, you've learned that you have the ability to receive guidance on any topic imaginable. Developing your intuition and using it consciously is truly empowering, as it frees you from the restrictive and stereotypical rules of society, and allows you to receive personalised guidance on creating *your* personal formula for success.

Chapter 13
BECOME A MESSENGER OF HEAVEN

From a very young age I had a strong and unexplainable affinity with fairies, unicorns and other mythical creatures. I loved drawing them, reading about them, and watching films about them. My room in Cyprus is filled with fairy and unicorn figurines and paintings, and as a young teenager I spent hours in flower shops and gardens fantasising about the little fairies that lived inside them. In school, Greek mythology was one of my favourite subjects, and I would lose myself in Odysseus' adventures as he battled the Sirens, the Minotaur, and other Greek deities.

As I got deeper into spirituality and metaphysics, and familiarised myself with the basic concepts and modalities, I couldn't help but wonder whether my teenage daydreams of fairies, unicorns and dragons held any truth. To my amazement, I discovered that not only did all these mythical creatures exist in real life, but that there are metaphysical modalities dedicated to studying and communicating with them. The idea of fairies fluttering merrily around my head and angels bathing me in their light was thrilling beyond imagination, and so, channeling – the metaphysical art of communicating with Spirit – was a road I had to take.

Aspects of God

The books I read suggested that angels, fairies, and other spiritual beings worked closely with humans to guide them in following and succeeding in their life purpose. There were entire chapters dedicated to all the different archangels, along with special prayers and techniques for communicating with them. Although it was fun reading about the subject and trying out these techniques, I couldn't help but notice their contrast with a piece of knowledge that I came to believe unequivocally through personal experience – the concept of Oneness, as discussed in Chapter 4.

If we are all connected to the One stream of consciousness that is God, and we are physical extensions of that stream, why bother to communicate with angels and fairies? Why not communicate with God directly? Furthermore, how does the belief in all these different spiritual beings relate to the concept of Oneness?

My prime sources of knowledge for the characteristics of the different magical realms were Doreen Virtue's books and meditations. Doreen Virtue is a spiritual doctor of psychology and a metaphysician who is famous for her work with the angelic, elemental and ascended-masters realms, and she is one of my favorite metaphysical teachers. When I found out that I would have the chance to interview Doreen[4] as part of her UK blog tour in 2012, I immediately took the opportunity to exclaim my concern to her. Her response confirmed what I was getting intuitively about the subject.

Spiritual beings, like angels, fairies, unicorns, mermaids and dragons, are all different *aspects* of God, which are connected to the single stream of consciousness that we are all part of. In the same way that we are physical extensions of God in a three-dimensional world, there are all kinds of beings expressing in different ways, which have their own unique perspectives and purpose. In the same way that we have our personal and collective purposes on this planet, they also have their own. The fairies' purpose involves nurturing the natural world; the angels act as messengers of the unconditional love that is God; and unicorns bring out the purity that is the basis of our existence.

Working With Humans

While personally working with spiritual beings, they have communicated that they choose to work with us because we are creators of consciousness. With every thought, desire, and experience that we have we create

---

[4] To read my interview with Doreen Virtue visit www.georgelizos.com/blog/doreen-virtue.

something new, because we bring forth something that's never occurred before. As discussed in Chapter 4, we've gone from living in caves and feeding on raw meat, to living in megacities and delighting in haute cuisine. The reason we chose to be physical, as opposed to spiritual, extensions of God, is so that we could be universal workers for expanding consciousness. We have an important mission here, and all spiritual beings are willing and honoured to help us to succeed.

The reason we may choose to work with spiritual beings, rather than God directly, is because spiritual beings vibrate at a frequency closer to ours, so it's easier to hear them. Our ability to focus our thoughts allows us to stray away from our natural, high-vibrational state of love and happiness, where God resides. As a result, when we feel low we don't have access to God, and we need God's messengers to show us the way back home.

But even when we are fully aligned to God, we may choose to work with other spiritual beings instead. Being physical beings, we love labels. It's easier for humans to conceptualise something that has form and personality, rather than talk about some invisible force with no form, gender, or other characteristics. Although we may understand that, in essence, we are all One stream of consciousness, we are still individual personalities in individual bodies. In this respect, it feels more real when we personalise God, or compartmentalise it into angels, fairies, and unicorns, to represent God's different aspects.

The fact that we do that doesn't make them less real though, for spiritual beings are eager to work with us in any way we like. In other words, whether you choose to channel God, angels, mermaids or any other form of being, you are always having a communication with the One stream of consciousness that is God, because they are all part of it.

Degrees of Alignment

As mentioned in the previous chapter, the more aligned you are to Source, the more access you have to Its wisdom, and therefore, to intuitive guidance. As a rule of thumb, the stronger your alignment is to Source (your Divine Self), the more access you have to all sorts of spiritual beings.

On the other hand, your misalignment with the vibration of your Divine Self restricts you from receiving intuitive guidance, and communicating with spiritual beings. Fortunately, you can never misalign yourself to such an extent that you have no access to Source, because you are literally made out of it. For this reason, you always have a direct access to it whenever you need it. This is what the guardian angels are here for. No matter how discordant you are from love, you always have a guardian angel by your side, pointing you in the right direction.

As discussed in the previous chapter, communicating with Spirit is an innate skill that everybody has. Little children do this all the time, but lose their ability as they lose their alignment, and as their parents dismiss their experiences as fake. In this chapter, I will guide you in further developing your intuitive abilities so that you can communicate with all kinds of spiritual beings, including your departed loved ones. They are all here, in different dimensions, trying to catch your attention and provide you with their guidance; you just need to train yourself to receive their messages.

Your Spiritual Guides

Your spiritual guides are spiritual beings who choose to work with you over a period of time. Some of them stay with you for your entire life, like your guardian angels; and others come and go according to your desires, life experiences and purpose. Connecting with your spiritual guides is an uplifting experience, for they always see you for the magnificent being you really are, activating your potential and minimising your self-perceived limitations. As a result, communicating with them affords you unlimited encouragement and guidance to follow your dreams and thrive in your life purpose.

The following list includes the most common types of spiritual guides people come across when they venture into the non-physical world. These spiritual beings are especially significant, for they have worked with humans since antiquity. As a result, they have certain personalities and characteristics, as well as specific purposes in their interaction with humans.

Angels

The word angel means "messenger" in Aramaic and Greek, since angels are the messengers of God's love and light to humans. These holy beings work closely with humans, the Earth, and the Universe, to assist us in raising our vibration to the energy of love. As a result, the angels are adept at healing any emotional, mental, physical, or spiritual imbalances that you have, and help you transcend them into love. They are usually experienced as radiant, pulsing beings of light in various sizes, their wings of light extending outwards to every part of the Universe.

The angelic realm consists of a wide range of angels, each type with a different purpose. These are the Seraphim, Cherubim, Thrones, Dominions, Virtues, Power-Bearers, Archangels, and Guardian Angels. The ones you are most likely to encounter are the guardian angels and archangels, who work closely with humans. Archangels are unlimited, multidimensional beings who can help many people at the same time, and each one has a unique set of characteristics and topics of interest. On the other hand, guardian angels are personal to each human being. We all have at least two guardian angels constantly with us, ready to help when asked to.

Fairies

Fairies encompass a vast category of nature spirits, ranging from mermaids, dragons, djinns, dwarves, pixies and flower fairies, and work with the four elements of Air, Fire, Water and Earth. The fairies are the spirits and consciousness found inside everything natural. As a result of their closeness to the earth and humans, they are great for offering practical guidance on human topics such as relationships, careers, and finances. In contrast to the angels, fairies have an ego and demand to be respected, so you'll need to earn their trust first before they sprinkle you with their fairy dust. Being nature spirits, they cherish the environment, and expect people to do the same.

Unicorns

A unicorn is a magical horse with a horn, the alicorn, coming out of its forehead. These are pure, gentle and beautiful magical creatures representing spiritual virginity and purity of heart. They have been historically understood to be unruly creatures of male primal power that cannot be tamed, but can be baited by a young virgin girl. The purity of their nature makes unicorns suitable for helping you reconnect with your inner child and your true, loving self, as well as give you the courage and strength to express your individuality. According to Diana Cooper, unicorns are the guardian spirits of people who have a global life purpose – hence, people whose purpose involves making a significant positive contribution to the world.[9]

Totem animals

A totem or power animal is a spiritual guide in the form of an animal, representing a person's qualities of character, power and personality, and is said to accompany a person throughout his entire life. The totem originated in Native North American tribes, and Shamans who had totem animals as spiritual guides for their clans, as well as on an individual basis. I personally see my totem animal as a very personal spiritual guide who knows my true passions and desires, and is synonymous with, as well as an extension of, my higher self. Finding your totem animal is like finding the twin brother or sister you've never had, a best friend, and a lover, all in one.

Dragons

Symbolising power, strength and leadership, these fire fairies are misunderstood spiritual guides, usually presented as mean and evil monsters in the bulk of western folklore. As a result of the persecution of dragons in western history, they came to symbolise bravery and thriving through struggle. Because of this, dragons usually appear as the spiritual guides of people who are inherently strong and dynamic, but have compromised their nature for the sake of society's set rules and stereotypes. The dragons are great mentors, and provide unlimited bravery, helping you own your authenticity.

Mermaids

Also part of the fairy realm, mermaids are the spirits and consciousness of the ocean. Just like the depth of the ocean, mermaids help you get in touch with the depth of your unconscious mind, and heal repressed fears and beliefs. Mirroring our association of the sea with romance, mermaids are adept at healing and harmonising your romantic relationships, as well as your relationship with yourself. As inherent symbols of hybridity, mermaids also remind you of your own spiritual hybridity, as a half-physical and half-spiritual being.

Departed humans

It is believed that we all have at least one departed relative or friend with us as a spiritual guide. These spiritual guides are different from the ones mentioned before, in that they used to be human beings with a distinct personality, characteristics and ego, and we've had a physical relationship with them. Channelling your deceased grandmother or friend can be very beneficial, since they deeply care about you and will always give you heartfelt advice.

Touched by an Angel

My first experience with the spiritual world was in my mid-teens, after I read an article about meeting my guardian angels. I had learnt about angels in Sunday school when I was younger, but it never crossed my mind that I could communicate with them in a way other than praying. Being raised as a Greek Orthodox Christian, I was brought up into an environment that encompassed hundreds of different saints, as well as Archangels Michael, Raphael and Gabriel. I remember going to church and praying to all the different saints like everybody else; but as far as I was concerned, praying involved mentally asking for favours, and hoping that they would offer a helping hand – and most of the time they did. I never thought that it would be possible to actually have a conversation with them.

Therefore, when I found out that there was a way to communicate with Spirit, I was intrigued. The article instructed me to sit in meditation and ask my guardian angels to give me a sign that they were with me, in a way that I would understand. Even though it seemed overly simplistic and childish, I went with it and mentally asked my guardian angels to send me a visual message of their presence. A few minutes of no palpable sign later, I came out of meditation and went on with my day, doubting that anything would happen, but hoping something would.

A few days had passed without any palpable sign, and just before I discarded the whole thing, the anticipated sign came in the most unexpected way. I remember walking into the kitchen to get some water when I spotted something on the floor. I looked down to find a beautiful white feather lying right in front of me. I was bewildered! I now know that the angels had probably given me many more signs before that point, but I simply couldn't see them due to my untrained intuition. So, they had decided to be blunt and explicit.

From that day onwards I was certain about my guardian angels' existence, and I pledged to learn how to best communicate with them and follow their guidance. In the months and years that followed, I took meditation courses, received training in channelling, and read every book I could get my hands on about them. I was hooked on my invisible friends, and what I could achieve with their guidance. Whenever I was in trouble, or simply needed a sympathetic, non-judgemental friend, I would go into meditation and ask for their advice, or simply talk to them in my head. I knew that I could never be alone, for I always had my guardian angels by my side.

Communicating With Your Spiritual Guides

A common problem many people encounter when they first engage in channelling, myself included, is fear of the unknown. This fear is rooted in the belief in evil spirits and spiritual possession, which is mostly propagated by Hollywood films. In truth, there is no such thing as a source of evil. What many people experience as evil spirits are just negative thought-patterns created by other people's fear and negativity. Being thought-patterns, they have no agency and cannot harm you in any way – only scare you.

There is only a source of unconditional love, and you are a direct expression of it. Any experience of evilness is a result of your misalignment with your Divine Self. Therefore, the more aligned you are with Source, the less experience you will have of unwanted thought-patterns and negativity.

To help you navigate the Spirit world both safely and effectively, I've designed these two channelling techniques:

1. *Channelling through meditation*

   i. Get into a meditative state. This will allow you to raise your vibration to the frequency of Source, so that you can best facilitate the communication with your spiritual guides.

   ii. Shield yourself by using the psychic shielding technique provided in Chapter 9. Call upon Archangel Michael and ask him to strengthen your shield, and guide you through this channelling process. This will protect you from any form of negative energy.

   iii. Mentally and consciously, ask your spiritual guides to send you a sign that they are present, in a way that you will understand. This is important, for every person receives information and understands signs in different ways. It is important that you read Chapter 12, and familiarise yourself with how to best use your intuitive abilities to receive these signs.

iv. After you've received a clear sign, mentally ask your spiritual guides to reveal themselves, if they haven't already. Don't make things up; just stay calm, keep your mind clear, and release physical tension. Eventually, you will start noticing the presence of beings around you. They will appear to you according to your dominant intuition languages. If you get tense or scared, simply affirm that "Only love is real," and ask Archangel Michael to protect you. As the fear goes away, your guides will make themselves fully present. They may appear to be angels, fairies, unicorns, mermaids, saints, animal spirits, gods and goddesses, or any other form that means something to you. Your guides will always appear to you in ways you can make sense of, and associate with, so don't be surprised if your guide appears to be a gladiator, a teddy bear, or even a bug. Source is limitless, and your spiritual guides will work with whatever you can relate, and feel safe with.

v. Having familiarised yourself with your guides, you can ask them any question that you want. When I first met my guides, I started with asking their name, as well as their specific purpose in working with me. I realised that each one had a unique personality and perspective, as well as a different interest in me.

vi. At the end of the channelling session, thank them for communicating with you, and ask them to remain by your side, guiding you through your life.

Go through this process whenever you feel emotionally depleted, or whenever you need support with your goals and purpose. Your guides will always be there as loving listeners and wise teachers, to provide you with accurate guidance.

2. *Channelling through automatic writing*

Whereas channelling through meditation is useful when you first meet your spiritual guides, the concept of visualisation and meditation gives your ego permission to doubt what you experience, rendering it fake and a product of make-believe. Channelling through automatic writing is a more objective method, which can help you deepen your relationship with your guides.

As its name suggests, the only thing you'll need to practise automatic writing is pen and paper, as well as your alignment with Source. Automatic writing, or drawing, involves asking a question and allowing your spiritual guides to give you the answer intuitively in words or drawings. During automatic writing, you literally allow your spiritual guides to flow through you, to blend with your consciousness, and express their message. These always come as intuitive impressions, through your dominant intuition languages.

Unlike the concept of spiritual possession, with automatic writing you have full awareness and control over your entire being, and *you* are responsible for translating the guidance in written words. To practise channeling through automatic writing, do the following:

i. Follow the first three steps of the *Channelling Through Meditation* process.

ii. Get a piece of paper and jot down a question you need guidance on.

iii. Stay relaxed and keep your mind unfocused. Allow your hand to write or draw freely. Everything that comes into your mind, from the point where you state the question onwards, is part of the answer. Channelling in a question-answer format like this makes communication with your spiritual guides more clear and objective, because it allows you to separate your personal questions from your guides' answers.

iv. End your automatic writing by thanking your guides, and asking them to guide you and protect you in your path.

Alternative Ways of Communication

Channelling is not the only way to communicate with your spiritual guides. Simply asking for help will also do the trick, since your guides are constantly with you, always trying to catch your attention so that they can provide their guidance. When it comes to getting answers to specific questions, mentally asking the question is still sufficient, but you need to be mindful enough and aligned enough to receive your guides' answers through your intuition.

Through the ages, people have used a plethora of tools and modalities to communicate with their spiritual guides. From sacred rituals, sacrificing animals and constructing altars, to using crystal balls, tarot cards and other divination systems, human history is filled with thousands of ways to lift the veil of the spiritual world and communicate with Spirit. However, in the modern society we live in, it would be impractical to undertake some of the above methods.

As a result, I've simplified some and modified others, to provide you with the following fun and alternative ways of communicating with your spiritual guides:

1. *Build a mini altar*

When I was younger, I became enthralled with the earth-based religion of witchcraft. What I loved most about it were the elaborate altars which formed the basis for its practice. Ever since, I was fascinated by the idea of building an altar in my room – a place that I could decorate with statues, symbols, candles, incense, and all kinds of magical tools I'd read about in books on magick and witchcraft, to honour and communicate with the spirit world. The only problem with such books was that they instructed a very specific assortment of tools and items, which where usually expensive to purchase, and which I could only find online. Most importantly, even though I respected the faith of witchcraft, I had no desire to convert.

In time, I realised that an altar was supposed to be a much more personal space than that: a place that symbolised my personal belief system, as well as my connection to my spiritual guides. Therefore, it would be more appropriate to adorn it with objects and symbols that captured the essence of that connection.

Constructing an altar is a beautiful way of nurturing and strengthening your relationship with your spiritual guides, as well as communicating with them. An easy way to do this is to collect objects, colours, symbols, flowers, crystals, pictures or anything that symbolises your connection with your guides, and place them together somewhere in your room or house. It's important that you create the altar in a room where you spend a sufficient amount of time every day. Your connection with your guides is inherently intimate, and so should your connection to your altar be.

Creating an altar has the effect of bringing your spiritual guides, and your relationship with them, into life. Bringing them into your everyday space, your spiritual guides cease being the invisible beings you talk to in your head, and become embodied in your life through the symbolism you have created. Whenever you need your guides' assistance, light a candle on your altar, and trust that your spiritual guides are doing everything they can to be of assistance.

2. Use oracle cards

Oracle cards and tarot cards have become increasingly popular. I personally find the use of cards to be the easiest and most practical way of communicating with my spiritual guides. The idea behind oracle and tarot cards is that you ask a question and your spiritual guides choose the most appropriate cards in the deck to provide you with their guidance.

However, there is still some level of interpretation required, since pictures, symbols, and even words have different meanings to different people. I've never trusted symbol and tarot dictionaries, for I know that our subconscious mind works in a very personal way, so that a black cat may be a bad omen for one person and a good one for another. I have always believed in interpreting the cards in an intuitive way. This simply means being mindful of the way you feel when you draw a card, and using your dominant intuition languages to interpret its symbolisms.

If you have never used cards as a divination method before, then I would suggest that you start working with oracle cards first, before you move to tarot. This is because oracle card readings are much easier to do, as tarot readings require special training and practice. Several metaphysical teachers have published oracle card decks specific to certain spiritual guides, such as unicorns, fairies and angels. This makes it exceptionally helpful for your spiritual guides to express their messages in a more genuine way, since the card decks are created to support their individual nature.

3. *Interpret your dreams*

Our dreams represent one of the purest forms of communication with the spirit world, because when you go to sleep you cease thought and reconnect with your Divine Self. In that pure state, you have access to the infinite intelligence of the Universe, and you become a clear vessel for your spiritual guides to express through you.

During your sleep time, your spiritual guides are free to express themselves without the constraints of your ego. They express themselves through your emotions, images and personal symbolism. Therefore, the key to interpreting your dreams lies in interpreting the symbols in them, and relating them to the way you felt while having them. Although there are many different types of dreams, every single dream that you have contains messages from your spiritual guides, urging you to choose a path towards love and your life purpose.

The following four steps will show you how to interpret your spiritual guides' dream-messages accurately:

i. **Divide your dream into symbols:** For example, a dream where you got bitten by a dog at night outside your house can be divided into five symbols: The dog, getting bitten, the night, your house, and being out of your house.

ii. **Interpret the symbols:** Once you've divided your dream into symbols, ask yourself: What does this symbol mean to me? How does this symbol make me feel? In the example of the dog dream this could be: The dog symbolises friendship; the biting symbolises pain; the house symbolises being safe; the dark night symbolises the unknown; and being out of the house might symbolise not feeling safe enough.

iii. **Combine the interpretations:** Once you've noted down what each symbol means to you, it is easier to unveil the message behind the dream. For example, if you put together the symbolisms from the dog dream, you can say that it's about being bullied and victimised in a world that feels strange to you, even by you own "friends".

iv. **Consider your feelings:** You can tell if the interpretation you've arrived at is the true one by paying attention to your gut feeling, as well as the way you felt during the dream.

This method makes you fully equipped to analyse your dreams and receive messages from your spiritual guides. Your guides will take every opportunity they have to communicate with you, and your dreams provide a feasible framework for them to express their messages in their purest form. If you have specific questions you need enlightenment on, mentally ask your guides to provide you with the answer in your dreams. As soon as you wake up in the morning, take a piece of paper and jot down as much information as you can remember from the dream you last had, and then use the above steps to glean its messages.

Having a friend to talk to when your world seems to be falling apart is an essential step towards spiritual transformation, and it is in our nature as human beings to establish relationships and share our experiences in some way or another. I experienced loneliness at a time when I most needed someone to love me for who I was, and help me rise from the ashes. Just before I completely lost hope, I found out that I was never truly alone, as I was always surrounded by spiritual beings who loved me unconditionally.

Don't misunderstand me – I'm not suggesting that you break off your human friendships and hang out with angels, fairies and other spiritual entities. You are an earth-based being, and you are here to mingle with the others of your kind and experience life together. However, there do come times when you are deprived of emotional support from your earthly friends. At these times, guidance from above is always available, and utilising it is the brave thing to do, however wacky this can seem to you or others.

Chapter 14
YOU ARE THE GURU

In the pages of this book, you have awakened, nurtured, consolidated, and empowered the spiritual teacher that you are. You now don't just conceptually know about the qualities of being the guru, but you have actually experienced them. You are equipped with a toolkit that you can use to venture into your own spiritual transformation, and follow your life purpose fearlessly.

This is the ultimate form of self-empowerment!

You are no longer dependent on other people for wisdom, support and guidance, for you've learned how to be your own source of guidance. You may still enjoy reading books, taking workshops, attending seminars, and seeking others' guidance, but you are not dependent on any of these. They are merely complementary resources to help you develop your own voice and message.

The only person you are dependent upon is your own Self. Your alignment is your greatest weapon, and the only tool you need to be the guru and thrive in your life purpose. For this reason, in the closing of this book I will reiterate what I believe are the most important tools, tips, and concepts to help you sustain your alignment moving forward.

Your Spiritual Practice

My guitar teacher used to tell me, "When you abandon your guitar, it will abandon you too." Spirituality is very similar to that. When you abandon your daily spiritual practice, you'll eventually fall back into your old habits, and you'll lose your alignment. For this reason, there is nothing more important than having a daily spiritual practice.

As it always does, the ego will sabotage your spiritual practice by telling you that it's too silly, too easy, too ineffective, or that you don't have the time to do it. My dad always told me that "there is no such thing as *I can't*. There's only *I won't*." If you want to be your optimal self, and if you want to succeed in your life purpose, you will find the time and the energy to invest in your spiritual practice.

This book has provided you with a multitude of processes that you can use to restore your alignment. It is impossible to practise all of them daily, and I don't advise that you do. What you need to do is craft a personalised spiritual practice that you genuinely enjoy doing on a daily basis. Whatever you choose to do, it is important that you invest at least 15 minutes every day to do it, and you choose processes and activities that you genuinely enjoy, and which help you find your alignment.

Catch it Before it Gets Bigger

Negative emotion is a wonderful thing when you catch it early, and use it as an opportunity to learn something from it. However, prolonged negative emotion will eventually gain momentum and offset your alignment.

That's why, a crucial step in maintaining your alignment is having the courage to face negativity head on, before it proliferates. Your ego will want to stay rooted in blame, anger, and fear, and it's up to your willpower to overcome it, and use the tools you've learnt to eradicate it and regain your alignment.

How to Deal With Relapse

You *will* relapse. It is inevitable. You are a human being with an ego, and once in a while you will find yourself abandoning your spiritual practice and resorting to your old habits. In such circumstances it is vital that you do the following:

- **Don't judge yourself.** If you judge yourself and feel guilty for relapsing, you will only prolong the relapse and prevent yourself from rebounding. In one of her workshops, spiritual teacher Gabrielle Bernstein said that what's important "is not how often you relapse, but how quickly you come back home". Instead of feeling guilty, realise that you are no longer powerless against strife, and use the tools of this book to bring yourself home.

- **Start slow.** Once you regain your alignment, take small steps to get back to your daily spiritual practice. Don't overwhelm yourself with a full-blown one-hour practice – your being won't be able to take it. Instead, choose one process to work on for a week, and add on to that according to the way you feel.

- **Know that it'll get easier.** You will discover that the longer you commit to your spiritual practice, the easier it will be for you to maintain your alignment, and the less you will relapse. In time, your spiritual muscles will get stronger, your ego's hold will get weaker, and alignment will dominate your life. Your general level of happiness will reach such a high state that frustration will be the most negative emotion you experience, and nothing can throw you off your path.

Spirituality is Not a University Diploma

Many people mistakenly believe that spiritual awakening is like a university diploma – once you get it, it's yours for life. Unfortunately, this is not the case. Spirituality is a never-ending process of choosing love over fear, and keeping doing it. Abraham-Hicks capture the essence of spirituality when they say, "You can never get it wrong, because you can never get it done. And you can never get it done, because you can never get it wrong."

What they mean is that there is no end to life; and if there's no end there can never be failure, because you can always try again. This is such a liberating understanding, because it frees you from the need to be good and be perfect all the time. Life is an epic adventure, which is filled with both rewarding and challenging experiences. It would be too boring if all that you experienced was blissful and happy, for happiness feels so much better when you find it from a place of sadness. What's important is not that you eradicate all negativity from your life, but that you are conscious enough to be able to turn this negativity around, and align yourself to your Divine Self.

When in Doubt, Get on Your Knees

The most powerful spiritual tool I've provided for you in this book is the act of getting down on your knees in complete surrender. Surrendering, whether it comes from getting on your knees to pray, listening to a moving song, practising silent self-love, or any other way, is incredibly healing and liberating. When you have no idea how to deal with a life situation, when none of the processes you use work, and when nothing you try helps you improve your current situation, all you can do is let go.

The term "divine storm" is used to describe a situation where everything in your life crumbles down. You lose your job, break up with your boyfriend, lose all your money, become homeless – life as you knew it changes completely. What is divine about such an experience is that things can only get better. How many times have you read stories, or seen documentaries, of people who lost it all, and eventually rebounded with even more?

Sometimes the easiest path to transforming your life is to start with a blank canvas. If you fight against it, it'll only get harder. If you let go, the Universe will orchestrate the best possible circumstances to lead you to where you are supposed to go. I'm not saying that your life must crumble down to find your alignment and thrive in your purpose; but aspects of it may do, and if that happens, don't fight it.

Love is Your Destiny

Everything starts and ends in love, because everything is made out of love. You are literally made of love, and whatever life throws at you, you will be inclined to follow the path of love. Know this with all your heart, and trust that if love is your destiny, nothing can really go wrong. Accept this love as your truth, surrender to it, and allow yourself to melt into it. Be the presence and the source of this love, so much so that when you feel its power nothing else matters, everything is possible, and nothing ever fails. Living life from this perspective is the life of the guru.

KEEP YOUR GURU ON

Get weekly tools

Sign up to my email list to get weekly spiritual tools that'll nurture your inner guru and keep you on purpose at **www.georgelizos.com/signup**

Work with me

If you've enjoyed this book and want to go deeper, check out my spiritual life coaching programme and other courses at **www.georgelizos.com**

Become an Instant Manifestor

Take your manifestation skills to the next level with my self-study programme. Check it out at **www.georgelizos.com/instant-manifestation**

Stay in touch

Tell me all about your experience with becoming your own guru.

www.facebook.com/georgelizos
www.instagram.com/georgelizos
www.twitter.com/georgelizos

ACKNOWLEDGEMENTS

In the three years it's taken me to write and publish this book several people have provided their input and inspiration, knowingly or not:

Thank you dad for knowing how to push my buttons and get me to work, and mum for being a constant presence of love and support. Thank you both for being there for me through it all, and for always supporting my dreams.

Thank you Doreen Virtue for being a virtual motivational presence in my life. Your books and videos have instilled in me the courage and work ethic required to follow my life purpose.

Thank you to my best friends Valantis, Marianna, Katerina, and Elena for experiencing life in its entire spectrum with me. Your unconditional encouragement and unique perspectives have inadvertently shaped this book, and me.

Thank you to all the wonderful people who have helped bring this book to life. My friend and copywriter Polina, proofreader Stephen, layout designer Előd, and cover designer Fiaz for your creativity, and for enduring the endless revisions.

Finally, thank you Archangels Michael and Gabriel for being pillars of strength, courage, and inspiration through my life, and for guiding my spiritual journey since day one.

REFERENCES

1. Neale Donald Walsch. *Conversations with God: An Uncommon Dialogue, Book 1*. 1st ed. New York City. G.P. Putnam's Sons; 1996

2. Louise Hay. *You Can Heal Your Life*. Carlsbad. Hay House; 1984

3. Foundation For Inner Peace. *A Course In Miracles: Combined Volume*. 3rd ed. Mill Valley. Foundation For Inner Peace; 2008

4. Robert Holden. *Loveability: Knowing How to Love and Be Loved*. 1st ed. Carlsbad. Hay House; 2013

5. Esther Hicks. *Abraham-Hicks Publications*. www.abraham-hicks.com/ (accessed 26 May 2015).

6. Elaine N. Aron. *The Highly Sensitive Person: How to Thrive When the World Overwhelms You*. 6th ed. London. Element; 2003

7. Doreen Virtue. *Assertiveness for Earth Angels*. 1st ed. London. Hay House UK; 2013

8. Rhonda Byrne. *The Secret: The Power*. 1st ed. New York. Atria Books; 2010

9. Diana Cooper. *The Wonder of Unicorns*. 1st ed. Findhorn. Findhorn Press; 2008

ABOUT THE AUTHOR

Ben Hanley

George Lizos spends his days working for a popular metaphysical book publisher and spends his nights being a Spiritual Life Coach, both of which help him fulfil his life purpose of helping others find theirs.

He holds Bachelors and Masters Degrees in Metaphysical Sciences, a Bachelors of Science in Human Geography and a Masters of Science in Business Management. He is accredited by Doreen Virtue as an Angel Intuitive and Certified Realm Reader, and he is a Certified Reiki Master.

George runs a successful blog where he provides weekly spiritual tools to help people thrive in their life purpose, and features interviews with leading spiritual teachers. George is also the creator of *A Course In Instant Manifestation: A Step-by-Step Guide To Manifesting Your Desires Instantly.*

Originally from Cyprus, George now lives in London, where you'll usually find him planning and scheming for his next sunny excursion.

 @georgelizos    **/georgelizos**

www.georgelizos.com

Printed in Great Britain
by Amazon.co.uk, Ltd.,
Marston Gate.